MEDITERRANEAN SEA

Tanis

Pi-Ramses

Bubastis

FAIENCE TILE

Giza • Cairo

• Memphis

Saqqara

Faiyum Oasis

THE SINAI

HITTITE CHARIOT

Serabit el Khadim

EASTERN DESERT

Nile River

RELIEF FROM TEMPLE OF SETI I

QUEEN MERYETAMEN

Akhmim

RED SEA

RAMESSEUM

Abydos

Thebes

RAMSES II

Aswan

Elephantine Island

TEMPLE OF NEFERTARI

Abu Simbel

RAMSES II: MAGNIFICENCE ON THE NILE

**Library of Congress
Cataloging in Publication Data**
Ramses II: magnificence on the Nile / by the
editors of Time-Life Books.
    p. cm.—(Lost civilizations)
Includes bibliographical references and index.
ISBN 0-8094-9012-9 (trade)
ISBN 0-8094-9013-7 (library)
1. Egypt—History—To 332 B.C.
2. Ramses II, King of Egypt.
3. Egypt—Antiquities.
I. Time-Life Books. II. Title: Ramses the
Second. III. Series.
DT87.R34 1993
932'.014'092—dc20   93-26270

The Consultants:
David O'Connor is professor of Egyptology at
the University of Pennsylvania and curator-
in-charge of the Egyptian Section of The University Museum. In his comprehensive excavation of Abydos, Dr. O'Connor is exploring
the rise of Egyptian urbanism and the origins
of the pyramids.

Rita E. Freed, curator of the Department of
Egyptian, Nubian, and Near Eastern Art at
the Museum of Fine Arts in Boston, has participated in numerous Egyptian archaeological
expeditions. Dr. Freed also curated and wrote
the catalog for the exhibition "Ramses the
Great."

Kenneth A. Kitchen, professor of Egyptology
at the University of Liverpool since 1988,
with nearly 40 years experience in Egyptian
studies, has published numerous books and
papers and has lectured worldwide on the
Ramesside pharaohs.

The dates used in this book are based on
Dr. Kenneth Kitchen's high date chronology.

RAMSES II: MAGNIFICENCE ON THE NILE

By the Editors of Time-Life Books

TIME-LIFE BOOKS, ALEXANDRIA, VIRGINIA

CONTENTS

RAMSES, GREAT OF VICTORIES

His Majesty has built himself a Residence whose name is 'Great-of-Victories.' It lies between Syria and Egypt, full of food and provisions. The Sun arises in its horizon, and [even] sets within it. Everyone has left his own town and settles in its neighborhood." So reads a description, preserved on a 3,000-year-old papyrus, of ancient Egypt's lost capital—Pi-Ramses a Aanakhtu, literally "Domain of Ramses Great of Victories." It was a breathtaking, monumental city, altogether befitting its patron, Ramses II, more often known to the modern world by the exalted appellation Ramses the Great.

But unlike ancient Egypt's other two capitals, Memphis and Thebes—whose locations were never lost even when the civilization that created them had faded into obscurity—Pi-Ramses seemed, until quite recently, to have vanished from the face of the earth. Texts of that time indicate that the 12-square-mile city lay on the eastern side of the Nile Delta, along one of the great river's multiple outlets to the Mediterranean Sea. But where exactly among the papyrus marshes and flat, densely cultivated farmlands this imposing metropolis had stood remained hidden in history's shadows.

A showplace for large festivals, with its faience-tiled palaces, pillared chambers, and granite gates, Pi-Ramses was, according to the ancient texts, "beauteous of balconies, dazzling with halls of

With greatness yet to descend on him, a youthful Ramses takes a pensive pose. Like many Egyptian boys, he has a shaved head and a long lock over the right ear. Setting him apart from them is the royal cobra, conspicuous on his diadem.

lapis and turquoise." Its young men, they reported, "are in festival-dress daily, oil on their heads, hair freshly set. They stand by their doors, hands bowed down with foliage and greenery." Here were government buildings, mansions for high officials, warehouses piled high with grain, and temples to Re, Seth, Amen, and Ptah—the greatest of the Egyptian gods.

The rediscovery of Pi-Ramses began in the mid-1920s when peasants looking for salable artifacts began digging in a mound near the village of Qantir, some 60 miles north of Cairo. They found glazed tiles dating to the time of Egypt's 19th Dynasty, of which Ramses II had been the most illustrious pharaoh. The discovery suggested Qantir as a possible location of his lost capital. But the vestiges seemed scanty for so great a city, and when more substantial finds came to light at another site, about 15 miles to the north, attention quickly turned there.

The new material came from Tanis, where the French Egyptologist Pierre Montet had begun excavating in 1929. Among his many important discoveries over more than 20 seasons at the site were the tombs of rulers of Egypt's 21st Dynasty, who had made the city their capital in the 11th century BC. But there were also statues and monuments dating from Ramses II's reign 200 years earlier in such quantity as to suggest the city might have dated back to that time. The conclusion seemed to Montet to be obvious: Tanis and Pi-Ramses were one and the same.

Montet's theory, however, did not gain universal acceptance. In the late 1920s Egyptian archaeologists had begun excavating the mound at Qantir before it could be further looted. One of their number, Labib Habachi, deserves the credit for making a scientifically sound case for Qantir as the lost capital. In the 1940s he found steles at Qantir bearing inscriptions of Pi-Ramses and published his findings in 1953. Around a decade later, the Austrian archaeologist Manfred Bietak began a systematic exploration of the area

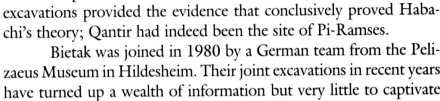

Massive fragments from a toppled statue of Ramses II are strewn amid the ruins at Tanis, in an evocative panorama (bottom). On the right, a giant foot treads before a fallen obelisk. The wall in the photo below is made of broken obelisks. These and other monumental pieces were removed from the city of Pi-Ramses after the branch of the Nile that linked it to the rest of Egypt silted up; they were transported 15 miles away to a new capital, built at Tanis.

where the peasants had discovered the tiles 40 years earlier. Bietak's excavations provided the evidence that conclusively proved Habachi's theory; Qantir had indeed been the site of Pi-Ramses.

Bietak was joined in 1980 by a German team from the Pelizaeus Museum in Hildesheim. Their joint excavations in recent years have turned up a wealth of information but very little to captivate the eye. Pi-Ramses, more than most archaeological sites, requires a good deal of imagination to see it as it once was. "We must picture the City of Ramses as a large urban zone subdivided by canals and lakes," says Bietak. "One can visualize a palace lake and several harbor basins that were connected to the main branch of the Nile through one or more channels." Extending over 12 square miles, the city possessed stout walls that may have once enclosed a chariot garrison, a parade ground, and workshops.

Elsewhere, as Edgar B. Pusch of the German team wrote in his excavation report, the diggers uncovered "samples of all sorts of metal pieces, cinders, blast pipes, as well as melting pots of various shape." To everyone's amazement, the archaeologists had exposed traces of a vast bronze-smelting works with furnaces almost 50 feet long—big enough to produce several tons of the alloy each day. No one had previously suspected such large-scale industrial production in pharaonic Egypt. Pusch believes that the installation employed around 300 metalworkers on a full-time basis *(pages 32-33)*.

Finally, modern archaeological research has provided a plausible answer to the confusion that surrounded the search for Ramses' city: Sometime near the very end of the 20th Dynasty, the rulers of Egypt decided to move their capital, perhaps because the branch of the Nile along which Pi-Ramses lay had silted up. The 21st-Dynasty founders of Tanis, for reasons of economy and expediency, chose to scavenge building materials from the former capital. They appropriated not only the stones of its temples but also the monumental obelisks and statues of Ramses to beautify their new city—possibly to link themselves symbolically with their lu-

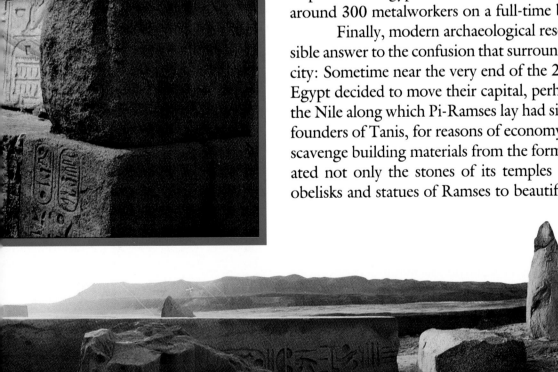

minous predecessor. These recycled materials, all of them bearing easily identifiable markings of Pi-Ramses, had led Pierre Montet to his erroneous conclusion.

Tanis was not the only city that used Pi-Ramses as a stone quarry; other nearby delta towns did the same. And countless generations of farmers have, until recently, gathered and crumbled the city's mud bricks to augment the fertility of the soil in their fields. As a result—and to the irreparable detriment of Egypt's archaeological record—Ramses II's dazzling capital, a city awash in history and power, was over time razed to its foundations.

The story of Pi-Ramses' rediscovery in some ways parallels the fate of its builder. Two centuries ago Ramses' very name was largely forgotten, remembered if at all from some passing and uncomplimentary references in the Bible. When in 1817 the English poet Percy Bysshe Shelley penned his sonnet "Ozymandias" as a commentary on the vanity of power, he took his inspiration from descriptions by ancient Greek and Roman travelers of a ruined statue lying near Thebes. The name Ozymandias is a Greek transliteration of the Egyptian title Usi-ma-re, "Strong in Right is Re," a name that was assumed by Ramses II on his accession to the throne. "Two vast and trunkless legs of stone / Stand in the desert," run the familiar lines. "Near them, on the sand, / Half sunk, a shattered visage lies. / And on the pedestal these words appear: / 'My name is Ozymandias, king of kings: / Look on my works, ye Mighty, and despair!' / Nothing beside remains. Round the decay / Of that colossal wreck, boundless and bare / The lone and level sands stretch far away."

Yet by a strange historical irony the forgotten ruler would have the last laugh. The fallen statue Shelley described—but never actually saw—is still there. Having outlived the poet, it may yet outlast the poem as well (page 48).

About a year before Shelley wrote his mocking verse, another colossal image of Ramses was being laboriously dragged from the Ramesseum—the pharaoh's mortuary temple at Thebes—to the Nile for shipment to the British Museum. In the following decades more and more statues, temples, and monuments constructed by the pharaoh would be uncovered. The deciphering of hieroglyphs enabled scholars to read the inscriptions chiseled into the walls of the buildings, providing detailed information on the ruler's almost 67-year reign. Gradually, Ramses II emerged from oblivion to take his rightful place among the great monarchs of history.

The culmination of this process occurred in the 1950s and 1960s with a United Nations-sponsored campaign to save the monuments of Nubia—above all the temples of Abu Simbel carved on Ramses' orders out of a cliff in southern Egypt—from submersion by the waters of the new Aswan High Dam. The rescue of these treasures was the most ambitious archaeological salvage operation in history and made the king's name and image familiar around the world *(pages 70-71)*. In 1985 and 1987, when an exhibition devoted specifically to Ramses II drew huge crowds in several U.S. cities, Ozymandias's revenge was complete. The "king of kings" whom Shelley had consigned to oblivion had become a media superstar.

The U.S. exhibition itself played a role in rescuing one colossal icon that construction workers had discovered back in 1962 while digging the foundation for a restaurant in the former Egyptian capital of Memphis. Experts recognized it as a giant statue of Ramses that must once have stood, like at least 10 other larger-than-life images of the king, outside the city's celebrated Temple of Ptah.

Money was lacking for this statue's restoration, however, until 22 years later when the mayor of Memphis, Tennessee, visited his city's Egyptian namesake in 1984 and expressed interest in showing the colossus during the Memphis stop of the upcoming Ramses exhibition. Egyptian authorities agreed, with the proviso that the statue be restored before leaving the country. Thirty conservators set to work refurbishing the 47-ton image of Ramses. Duly restored to its ancient splendor, the statue left its home of some 3,000 years—accompanied by an Egyptian military honor guard—and crossed the

The glazed ceramic tile below probably came from a floor or wall of royal living quarters—possibly the harem—in the palace of Ramses II at Qantir. On the tile a tilapia swims in water represented by zigzag lines. The Nile fish, which hatches its eggs in its mouth, symbolized rebirth.

Atlantic on shipboard to serve as the centerpiece of the show.

Not unexpectedly, there were shortcomings in the portrayal of Ramses that emerged from the dim past. Most of the information gleaned by archaeologists came from official records or inscriptions, and these texts conveyed only the image that the pharaoh himself chose to propagate. The inscriptions on the walls of his temples bear the record of his piety toward the gods and list his victories over Egypt's enemies but have little to say about Ramses the man.

Yet hints of Ramses' private life can now and again be glimpsed even in the monumental record. From the inscriptions it is learned, for instance, that in the course of his long life the pharaoh had at least half a dozen principal wives, fathered more than 90 children, and by the time of his death at the age of about 90 had outlived four successive heirs apparent.

Most sensational of all, the discovery in 1881 of his mummified body in a communal tomb, where it had been hidden from graverobbers in antiquity, revealed details of the monarch's actual physical appearance as opposed to the stylized public portraits that have come down through time. The investigators who unwrapped the body found a man about five feet, eight inches tall, with a long, thin face, a strong jaw, and a conspicuously beaked nose *(page 143)*.

Ramses II was born into a high-ranking, but nonroyal, family. At the time of the birth—the exact year is not known—his grandfather, whose name he inherited, held the title vizier, or chief minister, to the aging and childless pharaoh Horemheb. Aware of the dangers of a disputed succession, Horemheb had nominated his vizier as "Hereditary Prince in the Entire Land," thereby signaling his trusted adviser's role as heir presumptive. As such, Ramses' grandfather duly acceded to the throne of Egypt on Horemheb's death in 1306 BC, taking the title of Ramses I. He was not to enjoy supreme office for

Work in progress on a tomb in the Valley of the Kings for Horemheb, a general who had become pharaoh, shows red lines used to establish the proportions of figures, as well as corrections in black made over the sketch. A sculptor had already begun to carve the limestone wall, but for unknown reasons the tomb was left unfinished.

long, but when he died the following year, he passed the throne on to his son Seti I, whom he had brought up as a soldier. Seti's son, the future Ramses II, thereby became heir to the Egyptian throne.

The country Ramses would one day inherit already boasted a long and glorious history of some 1,700 years. On the walls of the temple Seti commanded to be built at Abydos in Upper Egypt, the pharaoh is shown—with Crown Prince Ramses—honoring a list of 75 earlier kings stretching back to Menes *(page 35),* believed to have founded the nation's First Dynasty around 3000 BC. The great early pharaohs were more than a historical memory to Seti and his contemporaries, for their monuments—including the pyramids of Giza, which were already more than a thousand years old in Seti's time— still dotted the landscape up and down the Nile.

Despite Egypt's relative isolation, with the sea to the north and desert buffers to the east and west, the nation's history had not been without conflict and setbacks in the intervening centuries. A time of internal troubles brought the Old Kingdom of the pyramid builders to an end in the 22nd century BC. About 150 years later a strong ruler succeeded in reuniting Lower Egypt—the northern, delta lands—to the upstream territory of Upper Egypt, and a new period of peace and prosperity, known as the Middle Kingdom, began. By the 18th century BC, however, the Middle Kingdom in its turn crumbled into disorder, and this time the situation was further confused by the infiltration of chariot-borne invaders from western Asia. The newcomers, Semitic tribesmen who were known as the Hyksos, crossed the Sinai and seized control of Lower Egypt. For the first time since dynastic rule had begun, a part of the country found itself under foreign rule.

The situation was finally retrieved in the 16th century BC by the rulers of Upper Egypt. From the capital at Thebes, their armies marched northward until they had driven the invaders out of the delta and once again reunited the entire land. In so doing they inaugurated the New Kingdom, a period of growth and grandeur that was to be Egypt's golden age.

Under the early rulers of the ensuing 18th Dynasty, the nation's boundaries expanded both southward and up the Mediterranean coast. Egypt became an imperial power. In the south, a viceroy was appointed to govern Nubia, while the territory of the Levant— the coastal region of the eastern Mediterranean—was divided into three provinces: Canaan, approximating modern Israel; Upi, southern Syria around modern-day Damascus; and Amurru, or coastal Syria including such Phoenician cities as Tyre and Ugarit. Governors of these northern lands supervised the local rulers, who were allowed to retain office in return for their fealty and their willingess to pay tribute to the pharaoh. Meanwhile, to the west, Egyptian garrisons stationed at desert oases kept watch on Libya's restless tribes.

The empire reached its greatest extent under the warrior-pharaoh Thutmose III, who claimed sovereignty over all the land of the eastern Mediterranean up to the river Euphrates, not far short of Syria's present-day border with Turkey. A peak of prosperity was attained in the following century under the long tenure of Amenhotep III, who ruled from 1397 to 1360 BC. This pleasure-loving monarch dotted the land with monuments to his own majesty that included the great temple at Luxor, a colossal pylon gateway at Karnak, a huge memorial temple on the west bank of the Nile, and the mammoth statues of himself that awe-struck Greek travelers would subsequently call the Colossi of Memnon.

Although Amenhotep bequeathed a peaceful and united kingdom to his son of the same name, certain tensions underlay the surface calm. On the Syrian border Egypt found itself facing the reemerging power of the Hittite kingdom, whose fortress capital of Hattusas lay some 3,000 feet up in the Anatolian tableland of what is now north-central Turkey.

Internally, too, the priests of Egypt's principal god, Amen, represented a potential challenge to the pharaoh's power, for the divine master they served was increasingly viewed as more prominent than the earthly ruler himself. Amenhotep, who had done much to boost the cult of Amen with his spectacular building program, also sought to minimize the attached risks by ensuring that the god's attendants remained strictly subordinate to the pharaoh's command.

Amenhotep's heir was to attempt a much more radical solution to the problem, and in so doing he would come close to tearing the country apart. Traditionally the people of Egypt had worshiped many gods, of which Amen, Re, Ptah, and Seth were the most powerful. The new pharaoh provoked a national trauma by rejecting the entire pantheon in favor of a single, omnipotent deity—the Aten, the sun's disk. In its honor, he changed his own name from Amenhotep IV to Akhenaten, "Effective-for-Aten." In order to distance himself still further from the priests of Thebes, he built a new capital roughly halfway between Memphis and Thebes, which he called

Akhetaten. There he could worship the new god in unroofed temples open to the sun's life-giving rays.

While the nation tried to absorb the shock of this cultural revolution, Egypt's northern rivals were growing stronger. Border regions in Syria, aware of the discord brewing along the faraway Nile, switched allegiance to the geographically closer Hittite kings, who were less absorbed with internal problems.

Akhenaten's death in 1351 BC created a crisis over the succession to the throne. Having no male offspring, Akhenaten was followed by Smenkhkare, possibly his brother, who himself died after about three years on the throne. At a time when the nation—still in shock from the theological upheaval—badly needed a steadying hand at the helm, supreme power passed to what may have been a third brother, the young Tutankhamen. Meanwhile Egypt lost northern Syria to the Hittite foe.

After Tutankhamen's early and childless death, the throne passed out of the royal family entirely into the hands of military men. First the short-reigning Ay, then Horemheb struggled to undo the damage to regal authority that Akhenaten's policies had wrought. They reinstated the worship of the old gods, whose rehabilitation had already been started in Tutankhamen's brief reign. Horemheb also did much to reestablish Egypt's authority beyond the nation's frontiers by launching raids into Nubia and Syria that demonstrated Egyptian might in areas from which it had been conspicuously absent in the previous decades.

On Horemheb's death, another soldier, Ramses I, inherited a land that was regaining its stability after the shocks of a period of revolutionary change. Ay, Horemheb, and Ramses I all had one thing in common: They were not of royal birth. As self-made men, they sought to reinforce—and legitimize—their right to be pharaoh by stressing loyalty to time-honored ways. These rulers had neither sympathy nor respect for the memory of Akhenaten—"that criminal of Akhetaten"—whose reign they viewed as nothing less than a national catastrophe. They also strove to discourage factionalism by emphasizing their own might.

Ramses I became the founder of the 19th Dynasty after Horemheb's death without an heir had brought the 18th Dynasty to a close. Ramses sought first and foremost to continue the healing process at home and to restore Egypt's tarnished imperial prestige abroad. In addition, he produced an heir, Seti I, providing the coun-

DOROTHY EADY AND HER TIME MACHINE

Dorothy Eady might have had a normal English childhood had she not toppled down the stairs when she was three and been knocked unconscious. When she came to, she said she wanted to go home, which was strange, since she was *at* home. The place little Dorothy had in mind was the Egypt of the pharaohs, and forever afterward she would dwell there in spirit. Growing up with a passionate interest in all things Egyptian, she contributed her services to the British Museum, became adept in hieroglyphs, and married an Egyptian who took her to his country to live. Soon divorced, Eady stayed on, convinced that she had been a priestess in the time of Seti I, Ramses II's father, and had become Seti's lover. At night, she claimed, her astral body would travel back 3,200 years to visit him, or the pharaoh would come to her.

Settling eventually in Abydos, where Seti had erected a temple, Eady—who would be known as Omm Seti, mother of Seti, after the son she had given

birth to during her short marriage—showed a curious and correct knowledge of the temple and its rites. She became adept at ancient medicine and magic, taming cobras, casting spells, and curing various ailments. Believing herself to be empowered by psychic knowledge, she

helped archaeologists find the long-lost site of the temple's garden. Until her death at 77, in 1981, she passed her days as the temple's unofficial guide (she likened a visit there to a trip in a time machine). She died convinced she was at last joining her "very own people."

Eady stands before the image of the man she adored, Seti I, carved on the wall of his temple at Abydos. She worshiped here in the ancient Egyptian mode, even making offerings of wine, beer, bread, and English tea biscuits.

try some much-needed continuity in the transfer of royal power.

Ramses, mindful of his own path to the top, indoctrinated his son in the military sciences, and apparently the lessons took. Seti's autobiographical inscription on a wall of the hypostyle hall at Karnak was particularly intimidating: "His majesty exults at beginning the battle, he delights to enter into it; his heart is gratified at the sight of blood. He lops off the heads of the dissidents. More than the day of rejoicing, he loves the moment of crushing [the foe]."

Seti's own son, Ramses II, inherited his grandfather's name and his conservatism, as well as his father's soldierly predilection. Ramses was probably about nine years old when his father came to the throne of Egypt. Seti had married the daughter of a well-placed lieutenant of chariotry, so the future pharaoh gained a military tradition from both sides of the family.

Ramses' ancestral home was the eastern delta town of Avaris. Once the Hyksos capital, Avaris lay in a cosmopolitan part of Egypt, close to both the Mediterranean Sea and the vassal states of the Levant. It must have been thronged with merchants; one 19th-Dynasty text describes them sailing "downstream and upstream, busy as bees, carrying goods from one city to another, supplying him who has nothing." There was also immigrant labor, come to seek work in what remained the principal superpower of the day.

Like all well-born Egyptians, the young Ramses would have learned to read and write and would have received instruction in the nation's theology, literature, and history. Careful attention was no doubt paid to his physical development, too. Pharaohs were expected to excel in the military skills of chariotry and archery.

Ramses was still only in his midteens when his father, with thoughts of past disputed successions very much in mind, decided to install him as prince regent. Shortly after Seti's accession, the boy had been given the official title of "Eldest King's Son" and accorded the nominal rank of commander in chief of the army. The intention now was to establish beyond all dispute his right to the throne in case his father should die suddenly, perhaps on one of his military campaigns.

Concerns for the future of the dynasty no doubt also lay behind Seti's decision to provide the teenage prince regent with his own royal menage. And marriage came early: In the 10 years before his father's death, both his principal wives bore him at least five sons

AN OUTPOST OF EGYPTIAN IMPERIAL MIGHT
BURIED UNDER A MOUND OF SAND

With its empire extending north well beyond its borders, Egypt had need to guard the vital trade and military routes that linked the country to its domains. One of these was a highway running across the northern Sinai into today's Gaza Strip. Both Seti I and Ramses II maintained forts along its length. But though depicted on a wall at Karnak *(opposite),* their locations still eluded scholars. Then, in 1967, a serendipitous discovery led archaeologists to one of the fortresses.

The Israeli archaeologist Trude Dothan had become aware of the sudden appearance of Egyptian artifacts on the Jerusalem antiquities market, a sign that looters were exploiting an ancient cemetery. But where was it? Sand clinging to a clay coffin lid suggested a coastal location. As Dothan's detective work soon revealed, the objects had originated just south of Gaza. But the archaeologist could not proceed until she obtained permission for a dig, and several years passed before it was granted and she could commence.

Excavating in an arid area a mile from the sea, Dothan unearthed more coffins. With a site so promising, she probed ever deeper. By the time her work was over (it was interrupted by the Yom Kippur War), she and her teammates had eliminated a 43-foot-high sand dune. Close to the bottom of it they had come upon a late 13-century BC settlement, with workshops and quarters for artisans. Underneath they found still other remains, the ruins of a many-roomed palace and the foundations of an early 13th-century BC fortress, complete with a reservoir for drinking water. It was clear to the archaeologists that here at last was one of Seti's and Ramses' famed desert outposts.

Archaeologists pick away at sand covering a clay coffin. Though appearing largely whole, it was fractured; the pieces were borne up by sand that had seeped inside.

Dothan and colleague inspect drawings of the site they excavated. The ruins are of the fortress; the adjacent hole was once a reservoir and source of mud for bricks used in the construction of the fortification.

A wall at Karnak depicting the pharaoh Seti I's campaign against the Canaanites includes towered fortresses (see highlighted one), *most of them* with reservoirs, located on the coastal road to Canaan. Because of the presence of such fortifications, Moses and his followers may have chosen to stay away from the shorter coastal route on the exodus from Egypt and taken instead the southern—and far more difficult—way through the Sinai.

and several daughters, and other children are also known to have been born to certain of the royal concubines.

As prince regent, Ramses was gradually introduced to the responsibilities of the nation's highest office. He was 14 or 15 when he went on his first military campaign, accompanying his father to Libya to suppress a threatened revolt *(pages 28-29)*. The following year he took part in a major raid in the Syrian borderlands to revive the Egyptian presence in Amurru and seize the key stronghold of Kadesh, a town of great strategic importance on the Orontes River. Seti met success and Kadesh fell—but the gains were only temporary. After his armies departed, both Amurru and Kadesh reverted to their former Hittite allegiance, a denouement Ramses would not forget.

Ramses acquired his first unaccompanied command—to put down a minor revolt in Nubia—at the age of about 22. He showed his mettle by personally leading a chariot charge that routed the rebels, an event commemorated on the walls of a small rock temple he ordered to be hewn out nearby. Evidently, Ramses had taken his early military apprenticeship to heart, for on this expedition he brought along two of his own sons, aged five and four. His next assignment was to organize an ambush for Mediterranean pirates who had been rash enough to infiltrate the mouths of the Nile in search of plunder. The raiders' ships were seized, and the raiders themselves were forcibly conscripted into the Egyptian army.

When not occupied with military affairs, Ramses was delegated by his father to supervise quarrying operations at Aswan, where the granite for statues and monuments was mined. Like fighting, building was an essential aspect of a prospective pharaoh's duties. When Seti died in 1290 BC, Ramses, in his midtwenties, was well prepared for the throne, his mandate established. Both the country's and the energetic young monarch's prospects seemed bright.

First, though, Seti's body had to be laid to rest. Following pharaonic tradition, Seti had made arrangements early in his reign for the construction of his tomb and, just as important, a mortuary temple where he could be worshiped, thereby guaranteeing him eternal life. Both of these building projects took place on the west bank of the Nile across from Thebes: the temple on the edge of the river's green belt, and the subterranean crypt farther on in the bleak wadi known as the Valley of the Kings, where every one of the pharaohs since

A colossus of Ramses II in the Temple of Luxor (right) *bears on the back a broken pillar displaying the pharaoh's name in oval cartouches. The one at upper left begins with a disk of the sun god Re, later repeated. Below it is a jackal's head atop a staff, hieroglyph for powerful, next to a figure of Maat, goddess of truth.*

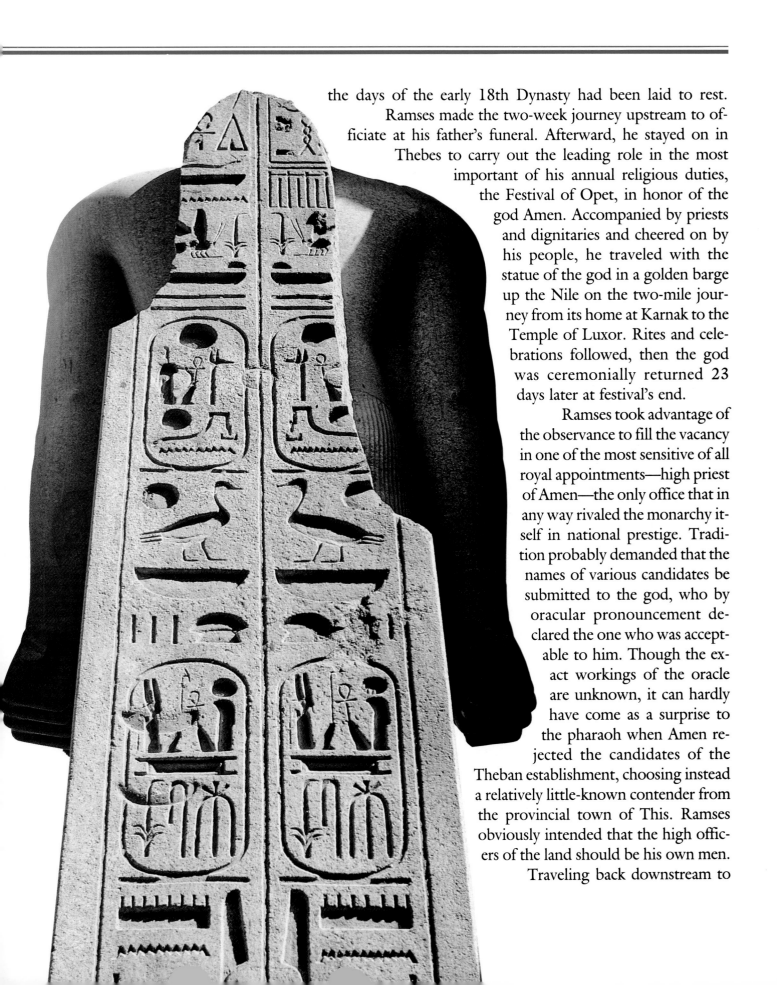

the days of the early 18th Dynasty had been laid to rest. Ramses made the two-week journey upstream to officiate at his father's funeral. Afterward, he stayed on in Thebes to carry out the leading role in the most important of his annual religious duties, the Festival of Opet, in honor of the god Amen. Accompanied by priests and dignitaries and cheered on by his people, he traveled with the statue of the god in a golden barge up the Nile on the two-mile journey from its home at Karnak to the Temple of Luxor. Rites and celebrations followed, then the god was ceremonially returned 23 days later at festival's end.

Ramses took advantage of the observance to fill the vacancy in one of the most sensitive of all royal appointments—high priest of Amen—the only office that in any way rivaled the monarchy itself in national prestige. Tradition probably demanded that the names of various candidates be submitted to the god, who by oracular pronouncement declared the one who was acceptable to him. Though the exact workings of the oracle are unknown, it can hardly have come as a surprise to the pharaoh when Amen rejected the candidates of the Theban establishment, choosing instead a relatively little-known contender from the provincial town of This. Ramses obviously intended that the high officers of the land should be his own men.

Traveling back downstream to

his northern residence, Ramses stopped off at Abydos to see how work on the second of his father's temples was progressing. He was shocked to find that construction had come to a halt. In the words of the inscription he subsequently had engraved on the walls, "Its monuments were unfinished, its pillars not set up on the terracing, its statue lay on the ground." He at once took matters in hand and gave orders for the work to be completed. He also took care that his filial piety in preserving Seti's legacy should be noted for posterity; the inscription went on to point out that "compassion is a blessing; it is good that a son should be concerned to care about his father."

The work at Abydos would form only a portion of an extraordinarily ambitious building program that was one of Ramses' chief concerns throughout his lengthy reign. For his construction projects, as well as for the conduct of all other endeavors within his kingdom, Ramses could count on the support of an elaborate and long-established officialdom with the pharaoh at its apex, the source of all authority and power.

In the day-to-day running of the government, the god-king traditionally delegated much of his authority to his two principal deputies, the viziers. One supervised Lower Egypt from the city of Memphis, sacred to the god Ptah; the other administered Upper Egypt from Amen's holy city of Thebes. The viziers' sweeping duties included arbitrating land claims, collecting taxes, maintaining public order, and meting out justice—apart from the pharaoh, only the viziers could condemn people to death. Depending upon the individual pharaoh's personality, viziers could, however, be kept on a short leash; an inscription in the tomb of Ramses' longest-serving vizier, Paser, indicates that, circumstances permitting, he was expected to consult daily with the pharaoh.

And the pharaoh could be a demanding taskmaster, as he demonstrated in the wording of a document known as The Installation of the Vizier. Archaeologists opening up tombs of high officials in the Thebes area found the text inscribed in no fewer than three of them, and it was quoted in part in a couple more, including that of Ramses II's chief vizier. By preserving this oath of office in his final resting place, each official seemed to be asserting that he had faithfully carried out his duties.

As the text reveals, the standards were high: "A magistrate's refuge lies in acting according to the regulations. A petitioner who has been judged should not be able to say: 'I have not been allowed

Delicately wrought of gold sheets over silver, then inlaid with glass, the pectoral above was found on the mummy of a sacred bull. Under Ramses' cartouche, a ram-headed falcon signifies the sun god Re, with whom the pharaoh was identified. Below the falcon, a winged vulture, symbol of Upper Egypt, grasps a red shen, *sign of rebirth and protection, while the cobra, emblem of Lower Egypt, designates power. In the bottom corners,* djed-*pillars stand for stability.*

to plead my innocence.' See equally the man you know and the man you do not know, the man who is near you and the man who is far away. Do not dismiss a petitioner before you have considered his words. Do not lose your temper with a man improperly; lose your temper only in a matter worth losing your temper over. Establish fear of yourself that you may be feared; for a real magistrate is one who is feared." In view of the strict accountability that was demanded, it is perhaps not surprising to hear the pharaoh's conclusion: "The viziership is in no way sweet; it is truly as bitter as gall."

Underneath the viziers stretched a complex pyramid of bureaucracy, from such high officials as the chiefs of the treasury and the granaries through the mayors who supervised provincial government down to local officials responsible for checking property boundaries and supervising the tithes of livestock and grain that filled the royal storehouses. At least on paper, tax collectors were encouraged to be fair and even indulgent in their dealings. "Do not be too severe," one text admonishes. "If the list shows very large arrears standing against the name of the poor man, divide it in three, and remit two-thirds." In practice, however, the authorities proved not always lenient or even honest. (Horemheb had at one point felt obliged to decree that those who abused their position would have their noses cut off.)

The temples and the army, which fell largely outside the viziers' jurisdiction, had their own hierarchies and answered directly to the pharaoh. The final pillar of the Egyptian establishment, the royal court, was even more the ruler's personal concern. Its high officials, though saddled with such fanciful titles as royal fan bearer or cup bearer, wielded substantial power through their personal influence with the monarch. Ramses looked to their ranks for candidates for many of the chief offices of state.

This entire elaborate administrative framework rested on the labor of peasant farmers, the overwhelming majority of the country's roughly three million people. For Egypt ultimately owed its prosperity and all its splendors to the slender, fertile ribbon of cultivable land—no more than a dozen miles wide and often substantially less—watered by the Nile. In good years, when the annual flood that resuscitated the fields was neither devastatingly high nor ruinously low, the great river provided not only food for those who worked the land but also an abundant surplus to sustain scribes and bureaucrats, priests and artisans.

The wealth of the nation was further enhanced by mining operations that provided turquoise from the Sinai *(page 55)* and gold from Nubia and the parched lands of the Eastern Desert. In good years, too, additional riches flowed in as tribute from the satellite states. Egypt had no coinage, relying instead on a complex system of barter to carry out business transactions, but its people

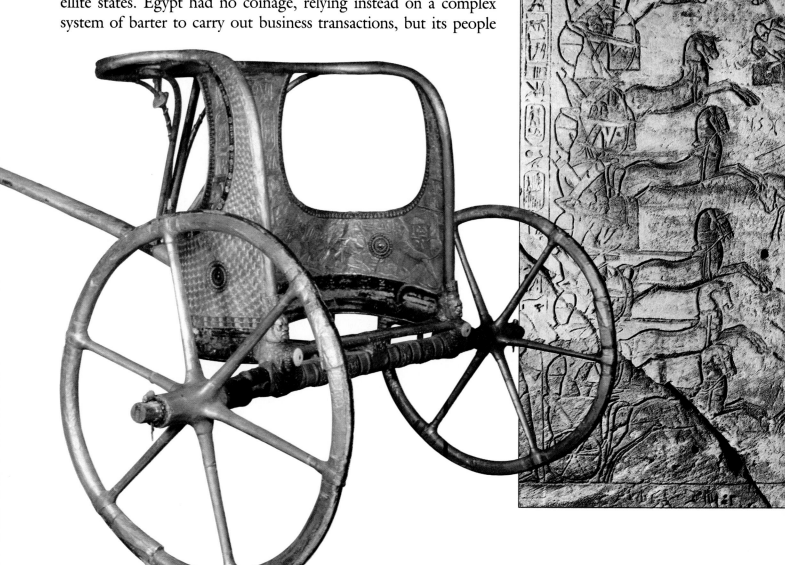

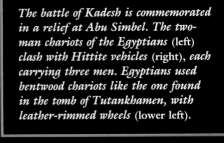

understood the concepts of wealth and poverty as well as any society of that or any other day.

With the nation's treasury replenished and its military standing again high after his father's successful rule, Ramses could look across the Mediterranean to the Hittite Empire, where there were old scores to be settled. In the fourth year of his own reign, the pharaoh finally felt ready to embark on an invasion of Syria—a move guaranteed to provoke war with the Hittites. His ambition seems to have been to outdo his father and to reassert Egyptian control over all the northern tributary states and in so doing to humble the Hittite foe.

In comparison with the millennial grandeur of the Egyptians, the Hittites were relative newcomers to the ranks of the great powers, having made their first appearance on the stage of history only about 600 years before. Even today scholars argue about where this stocky people originally came from. What is certain is that the language they spoke—a complicated idiom that took almost a century to decipher—belongs to the Indo-European linguistic family that includes present-day English. It was possibly the first such tongue to make its appearance in recorded history.

The Hittites owed their success partly to the facility with which they borrowed and adapted the new ideas and techniques they had met with on their migrations. Their military skills were particularly finely honed, above all their employment of chariotry. The Egyptians too had chariots, perhaps introduced by the Hyksos invaders. But while the pharaoh's army preferred a relatively light, two-man vehicle bearing just a driver and a warrior equipped with arrows and javelins for long-range fighting, the sturdy Hittite war chariot was a mobile fighting platform whose three-man crew included a shield bearer and a spearman as well as a driver. Hittite commanders used their chariots, which can still be seen depicted by Egyptian artists on temple walls at Luxor and elsewhere, as an assault force to batter their way through enemy lines, and they encountered few opponents capable of standing up to its onrush.

This was the opponent Ramses set out to confront in the summer of 1286 BC with a reliable and disciplined army of perhaps 20,000 men, organized into four divisions. Career soldiers, who devoted a lifetime of service to the pharaoh in return for a pension of livestock and land, provided skills and experience, while peasant conscripts filled out the ranks. The result was a well-trained force that could be called up at relatively short notice. In such cases, the pharaoh himself ceremonially supervised the distribution of arms from the state arsenals to the fighting men.

On Ramses' first campaign as pharaoh, his intention was not so much to confront the Hittites head-on as to reestablish the Egyptian presence in the Levant and to regain the territories lost since his father's last venture northward a decade and a half before. He and his troops swept through Canaan and into Lebanon, confirming the loyalty of the often restless subject peoples as they went.

Ramses' goal was the disputed province of Amurru. Facing the might of Egypt, its ruler, Benteshina, agreed once more to submit and pay tribute to the pharaoh. But once Ramses and his armies had departed, Benteshina made haste to contact the Hittite king, Muwatallis, in an effort to undo his enforced change of allegiance. Muwatallis had little choice but to respond to the provocation. The scene was set for an epic confrontation between the two superpowers in the next campaigning season.

Both sides made elaborate preparations for the coming encounter. Muwatallis called on the aid of allies and tributary states to raise what may have been the largest army the Hittites had ever assembled, numbering—according to Egyptian sources—37,000 men with 2,500 chariots. Ramses, too, commanded a huge force, made up of both Egyptian troops and captured sea raiders forcibly dragooned into the pharaoh's service. When Ramses finally set off northward in the early summer of 1285 BC, his scribes proclaimed that "all the foreign lands trembled before him, their chiefs bringing their tribute and all the rebels coming in homage through dread of his Majesty's might."

Fittingly, the scene of the encounter was to be Kadesh, long a bone of contention between the two empires. Without much thought to the strategic implications, Ramses decided to divide his army into two forces for the long trek north. He led the main force from Gaza by an inland route, riding ahead of his men in his glittering

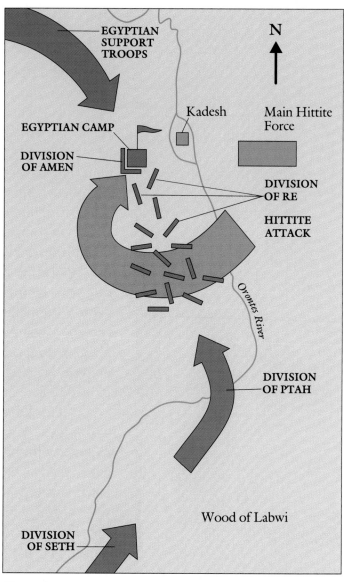

The above diagram locates opposing camps near Kadesh and the movements of contending armies. Arrows indicate the trek of Ramses' troops (purple) along the Orontes River, the sweep of the Hittite army (pink) as it broke through Egyptian ranks and overran their camp, and the path of Egypt's elite troops who came to the rescue of their countrymen.

war chariot. A support group was dispatched up the coast and was then to cut inland directly toward Kadesh.

Ramses must have been confident of his military strength, for he took few precautions on the journey, even though his scouts had failed to ascertain where exactly the Hittite army lay. As a result, he fell for a simple piece of trickery.

As Ramses approached the Orontes River just a few miles south of his goal, two Bedouin tribesmen joined the Egyptian advance party. They were taken to the pharaoh to be questioned about Hittite maneuvers in the area. Ramses was only too ready to take their word when they claimed that Muwatallis, fearful of Egyptian might, was skulking with his forces in the Aleppo region 120 miles to the north, not daring to risk a direct confrontation. This was a serious tactical error on Ramses' part, for in fact the men had been sent by Muwatallis to plant disinformation.

Unaware that he was heading into a trap, Ramses led the first of his army's four units, the Division of Amen, over the Orontes and onto the plain that lay before Kadesh. The rest of the army was strung out over many miles behind him. The pharaoh decided to pitch camp opposite the town. His men were busy unloading pack animals and oxcarts and putting up tents when an Egyptian patrol happened to capture two scouts sent out by the Hittite king. The captives were beaten to persuade them to talk, and they quickly revealed the truth: The Hittite army was encamped in battle array on the opposite side of the town, less than two miles away.

Ramses was furious. According to subsequent inscriptions, he railed: "So! The enemy are in hiding round Old Kadesh and neither my foreign chieftains nor my Egyptian officers with them knew anything about it." Messengers were dispatched posthaste to summon the other divisions of the army. Meanwhile Ramses called an emergency council of war. But while the pharaoh was still berating his staff, the Hittites struck.

What happened next—at least the Egyptian account of events—is well documented, because Ramses subsequently commemorated his own version of events in one of history's great exercises in state propaganda. He commissioned artists to devise pictorial descriptions of various scenes of the combat, which were then carved onto temple walls across Egypt. At Karnak and Luxor, in the new temples of Abydos and Abu Simbel, and at Ramses' own mortuary temple, the Ramesseum, the same scenes reappear. Meantime, an

From the series of reliefs in Ramses' temple at Abu Simbel commemorating some of his military victories, the scene on the left depicts the young king in his chariot, bow drawn, charging into Syrian ranks; the image on the right shows him smiting one Libyan while trampling another.

epic poem recounting the pharaoh's exploits was composed, preserving further details of the campaign.

Muwatallis sent his chariots across the Orontes. The strike force swept through the second Egyptian division as it was crossing the plain before Kadesh to join Ramses, then wheeled northward to attack the Egyptian headquarters. Reliefs show that the pharaoh's conference was rudely disrupted by horse-drawn warriors smashing a path through the fence of shields at the camp's southwestern corner. The Hittites were upon the Egyptians, and the great mass of Ramses' army was still miles away from the battlefield.

Disaster loomed, but what in fact ensued was Ramses' finest hour. The pharaoh leaped onto his own chariot and rallied his personal guard behind him. Then, showing great valor, he charged repeatedly into the foe. The Hittites were taken aback, the more so as, in the certainty of victory, some had unwisely dismounted to seize booty. Even so, the outcome of the encounter still hung very much in the balance when the Egyptian support force from the coast unexpectedly chose this crucial moment to arrive on the scene. Caught between Ramses' men and the newly arrived troops, the Hittite charioteers were forced to flee back toward the river, with the rallied Egyptian forces in hot pursuit.

What had promised to be a decisive Hittite victory turned into a rout. Two of Muwatallis's brothers died in the debacle, along with his secretary, the chief of his bodyguard, and several of his military commanders. Egyptian sculptors later gleefully recorded on temple walls one detail of the battle—a Hittite vassal, the prince of Aleppo, so nearly drowned in his haste to swim back to safety across the river that his own troops are shown unceremoniously upending him on the opposite bank to empty out the water he had swallowed. They also recorded Ramses' scornful comments on the lack of support he received from his followers in the moment of danger: "Not one of you was there, not one man to lift his hand to help me in my fight. I will not reward any man among you, for you deserted me when I was alone in the midst of my enemies."

Hard fought though it had been, the encounter had involved for the most part only the Egyptian and the Hittite chariotry; the main bodies of the armies had not been engaged. They were to meet the following day, by which time Ramses had had a chance to gather and organize his troops. Even so, he was unable to overwhelm the huge force that Muwatallis had gathered against him. After many

Photographed only days after its discovery in 1993, the tomb of Nakh-Min, Ramses II's overseer of chariots, messenger to foreign lands, and chief of bowmen, exhibits a cracked ceiling that must be shored up before archaeologists can venture into the sand-and-rubble-filled chamber beneath it. The walls are decorated with animal-headed gods and inscriptions from the Book of Gates, *a guide to the nether world.*

hours' fighting neither side had emerged victorious. At this stage Muwatallis chose to send envoys to suggest a cessation of hostilities, and Ramses and his commanders agreed.

Ramses was to use the fact that the Hittites had been the first to sue for peace to claim a great victory. But in fact when Ramses led his army back to Egypt, it was Muwatallis who was left in control of Kadesh. Moreover, he was able to strengthen the Hittite position in Syria by installing a puppet ruler in the disputed territory of Amurru. Then, striking southward, he went on to occupy the Egyptian province of Upi. None of this prevented Ramses from presenting the Kadesh campaign to his people as a glorious personal triumph. His claims might have occasioned some skepticism had fortune not come unexpectedly to his aid. Distracted by an unexpected challenge from Assyria, a rising power on the eastern fringes of his empire, Muwatallis proved unable to follow up his Syrian successes.

Ramses subsequently managed to restore the Egyptian position in the Levant. The lost province of Upi was regained in 1283 BC. In the following year, the pharaoh led his forces deep into Hittite-held territory north of Kadesh, prudently bypassing the city en route. A year later he again rampaged through northern Syria, showing courage and even foolhardiness at the siege of Dapur, where, according to an inscription carved on the walls of the Luxor and Ramesseum temples, he "spent two hours attacking the hostile Hittite city without wearing his coat-of-mail."

The Egyptians were able to carry out these campaigns with relative impunity because the Hittite Empire was now experiencing a succession crisis of its own. Muwatallis had died without leaving an obvious heir. The crown passed to the stripling son of one of his lesser concubines, who assumed office under the title of Mursilis III. But the young and untried monarch was largely overshadowed by his uncle Hattusilis, the nation's military strongman. There was distrust on both sides, and a standoff ensued. The result was that for fear of a palace coup Mursilis dared not leave his homeland to lead his armies in person against the Egyptians. The defense of the disputed lands had instead to be entrusted to subordinates.

Although Ramses thereby gained the tactical advantage, he in fact won little of substance from his Syrian adventures. When the Egyptian armies departed at the end of each campaigning season, conquered territories tended simply to revert to their earlier, pro-Hittite allegiances. The only way Ramses could have ensured their

DIGGING UP RAMSES' LONG-LOST CAPITAL

A wonder in ancient times, Pi-Ramses is cause for wonder again as a group of German archaeologists, led by Edgar Pusch, begin to lay bare the long-buried ruins of the pharaoh's great capital in the delta. The city had been created by Ramses apparently with the aim of moving Egyptian power closer to what was then the center of commerce in the eastern Mediterranean.

The finds are nothing less than sensational. Among them is a six-square-mile precinct—half the size of Pi-Ramses itself—designed as a battle staging area, with workshops, drilling fields, and stables for chariots in which the divisions stationed at Pi-Ramses may have also kept their horses.

At first the archaeologists found themselves puzzled by the Hittite materials they were uncovering at the site—lance and arrowheads, pieces of chain mail, and, more intriguing still, molds for hammering out metal fittings for shields like the Hittite one reproduced here as a backdrop. The Hittites, after all, had been Egypt's enemies for many years. But the archaeologists soon realized that these finds reflected the period of peace ushered in by a treaty between the two warring powers in 1270 BC and later symbolized by the union of Ramses II and a Hittite princess. Indeed, the objects—perhaps accompanied by workers with knowl-edge of advanced Hittite technology—might even have arrived in Pi-Ramses with the princess herself.

Yet another surprise came when the German team excavated smelters measuring almost 50 feet in length. Scholars had known from written and artistic sources, as well as intact artifacts, that the Egyptians knew how to cast metal, but none had ever dreamed that they were capable of producing metal on so grand a scale.

The smelters demonstrated clearly that at Pi-Ramses metalsmiths would have been capable of turning out several metric tons of bronze a day, more than enough to keep Ramses' troops well armed.

Archaeologists attempt to raise an octagon-shaped pillar in a foundry at Pi-Ramses. The huge furnaces, seen flooded by groundwater in the foreground, had high output, as evidenced not just by the size but also by scrap heaps and partially complete objects found in the area.

Egyptian water pipe in one hand, German archaeologist Edgar Pusch points with his other hand to a mold used in the manufacture of Hittite-style shields found at Pi-Ramses. The mold would have been used to shape bronze strips that would then be fastened to the edges of shields as strengtheners.

obedience would have been to install a permanent occupation force of the type that imposed peace in Nubia and, to a more limited extent, in Canaan. But for many reasons, such a solution was simply not feasible in northern Syria. Eventually the pharaoh seems to have realized the futility of further military effort; reports of the campaigns in Egyptian records quietly cease.

The situation was to change again in the following decade, when the conflict between Mursilis and Hattusilis finally erupted into civil war. Hattusilis emerged victorious and seized the throne, forcing his rival into exile. In this extremity, Mursilis turned to the old enemy of his country for help. He traveled to Pi-Ramses and asked the Egyptian pharaoh's assistance in regaining his throne.

Hattusilis now found himself in a dangerous position. With the Assyrians still a menace to the east, he faced the possibility of an invading Egyptian army—with Mursilis in tow and no doubt attracting the support of at least a portion of the Hittite people. Rather than risk military defeat, the old warrior decided to seek a peaceful solution. Quiet negotiations began between the two superpowers. Some 16 years after the battle of Kadesh, in the winter of 1270 BC, six Hittite and Egyptian royal envoys arrived at Pi-Ramses with the final agreement that would address the outstanding differences that divided the two nations.

By any standard, the peace treaty between Ramses and Hattusilis was an extraordinary achievement. Although specific borders were not mentioned in it, Ramses seems to have abandoned his claims to Kadesh and Amurru. In return, it was understood that Egypt was assured control over the eastern Mediterranean coastal lands and given access to ports as far north as Ugarit, in present-day Syria, where no Egyptian emmissary had set foot for more than a century. In addition, the two powers agreed to a mutual nonaggression pact, and each committed itself to come to the other's aid in case of attack by a third party. Another clause provided for the extradition of fugitives, specifying that those of lesser rank should be immune from prosecution on their return home. "Great men" were not accorded this privilege, perhaps because Hattusilis could not stomach the prospect of having to accord immunity to his rival, Mursilis.

The formal aspects of the treaty were almost as impressive— and ahead of their time—as its contents. The terms were carried to Pi-Ramses inscribed on a silver tablet. Papyrus copies were made for storage in the Egyptian state archives, and Ramses also had the treaty engraved on walls of the temple at Karnak and the Ramesseum, where they can still be seen to this day. To ensure observance of the treaty's clauses, the gods of each country were called upon as witnesses to the pact.

For years the Egyptian versions of the treaty remained the only ones known to scholars, and historians simply had to assume that similar copies must have been kept at the Hittite court. Then, one hot August day in 1906, a German archaeologist named Hugo Winckler who was excavating at Hattusas, the site of the Hittite capital, made a thrilling discovery. An assistant brought him a newly uncovered clay tablet. The tablet was inscribed in Babylonian—the international diplomatic language of New Kingdom times. Winckler was a specialist in ancient languages, and it did not take him long to realize that he was reading, almost word for word, the terms of Hattusilis's treaty with Ramses as recorded in hieroglyphic form on the walls of Karnak more than a thousand miles to the south. Some three millennia after the event, Winckler had found a Hittite copy of the treaty. It was, he later recounted, a moment as wonderful as a fairy story from *The Thousand and One Nights*; "all the experiences of my life paled into insignificance," he added.

As further proof of their commitment, the rulers exchanged letters of congratulations—as, in identical terms, did their principal wives. Official greetings were also sent to the Hittite court from the queen mother, the crown prince, and the vizier of Thebes. As Ramses watched envoys coming and going between the two courts, sweetening the negotiations with gifts of fine cloths and jewels, he must have felt a double satisfaction. In his conflict with the Hittites he had proved his might and valor as a warrior; now, through a conspicuous act of statesmanship, he could look forward to enjoying the fruits of a firmly established peace.

A MANSION FOR THE GODS

The pharaoh and his subjects lived in buildings constructed of brick and wood that have long since crumbled away. The temples of the gods fared better. They were built of stone, with eternity in mind. And this is why so many survive to the present day. Although most of them are in ruins, they still speak of time immemorial.

Among the greatest and most beautiful of these temples is the national shrine begun by Seti I and finished by his son Ramses II at Abydos, cult center of Osiris, god of the dead and vegetation. It was to this sacred spot, some 100 miles north of Thebes, famed as the supposed final resting place of Osiris, that worshipers flocked from all over Egypt.

Seti's choice of Abydos for his temple reflects the pharaoh's desire to bolster his legitimacy. His father, with whom the 19th Dynasty began, had not been of royal lineage, nor had his mother. What would be more to Seti's advantage than to connect his name with that

of the god whose worship seemed almost as old as Egypt itself? Under the pharaoh Akhenaten the ancient gods had been abandoned in favor of a single deity, the Aten. Now Seti could be seen restoring them—along with Osiris—to their former prominence in the new home he was erecting for them.

In order to make the most of the opportunity, the pharaoh had himself and his young heir, Ramses, portrayed on a wall of the shrine *(above)* standing before a long list of the kings of Egypt. (The impressive roll call dates back some 1,600 years to Menes, regarded as the unifier of the country.) By doing so, Seti firmly established his place in the lineup.

Egyptians regarded the pharaoh as the mediator between mortals and the divinities. If building the temple served Seti well, the deed would have pleased his subjects even more, for it was an invitation to the gods to smile again on Egypt and bless its inhabitants with long life and good harvests.

THE ISLAND OF CREATION

The architecture of Seti's temple, like that of all Egypt's temples, derived from the reed structure that myth claimed had been built on the primeval mound on which life originated. The mound, it was said, rose out of water and darkness to become the home of a divine falcon. To protect the falcon, a temple of reeds was built around it.

Following ancient convention, Seti's temple consists of forecourts and columned avenues that lead to a sanctuary area. Here seven small chapels echo, in their dimensions and rounded ceilings, the simple design of the original reed structure. Seti's scheme *(right)*, however, departed from tradition: It called for an L-shaped building, rather than a rectangular one. The wing, used largely for running the temple, apparently became necessary when a memorial dedicated to Seti and Osiris was built behind the edifice on ground that normally would have been given over to workaday rooms.

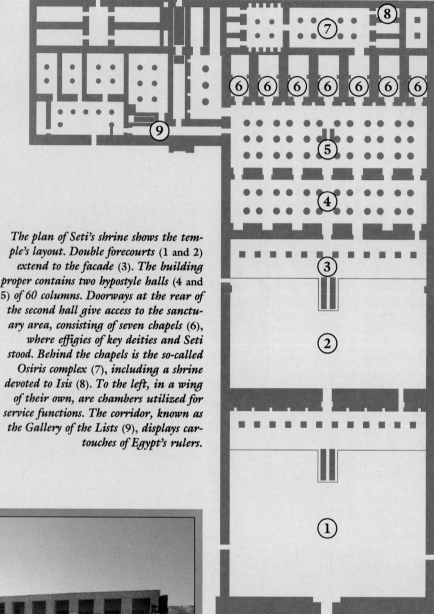

The plan of Seti's shrine shows the temple's layout. Double forecourts (1 and 2) extend to the facade (3). The building proper contains two hypostyle halls (4 and 5) of 60 columns. Doorways at the rear of the second hall give access to the sanctuary area, consisting of seven chapels (6), where effigies of key deities and Seti stood. Behind the chapels is the so-called Osiris complex (7), including a shrine devoted to Isis (8). To the left, in a wing of their own, are chambers utilized for service functions. The corridor, known as the Gallery of the Lists (9), displays cartouches of Egypt's rulers.

Seen from ruins of a pylon, Seti's temple is still imposing. The edifice was rebuilt in modern times after subsidence, brought on by the filled-in canal over which the shrine was erected, caused a collapse. The canal was probably used to float stones to the site.

Alternating images of Ramses II flank columns forming the temple's facade. Although the shrine was his father's, in finishing it Ramses glorified himself, even adorning the walls of the first forecourt with his victories.

IN A FOREST OF COLUMNS, WALLS THAT SPEAK

For the Egyptians, a temple was a living thing. Here wall reliefs and hieroglyphs delineated rituals that supposedly helped to keep Egypt from lapsing into the chaos that had prevailed before the primeval mound poked above the waters.

Not only did the faithful believe that humans were created, along with the original temple, at the so-called First Occasion but also that the dynamics governing the workings of the world—kingship, ethics, law, and religion—came into existence at that time as well. And since

all was perfect in the beginning, it behooved the pharaohs and priests to perpetuate the conditions that prevailed then by pleasing the gods through attentive worship and frequent offerings of food and wine. By inherent magic, even the stone reliefs showing piles of water fowl, slaughtered oxen, vegetables, fruits, and other delights were regarded as perpetual sustenance for the deities. "Come to this bread, which is warm," reads one inscription, "to thy beer, to these thy choice joints which the king has made for thee."

It is no wonder then that Seti and Ramses had the Abydos temple decorated from floor to ceiling with scenes showing the pharaohs in the company of the gods, carrying out numerous religious obligations. Seti and Ramses believed that they would be reborn as Osiris, become immortal, and be worshiped in turn. Thus it fell to the priests, after the rulers' deaths, to repeat the age-old rituals day after day, year after year, so that like the pharaohs and the deities themselves, society and Egypt might "exist unto the duration of the sky, forever and ever."

Just inside the first hypostyle hall, a relief shows Ramses II being purified by Thoth, god of wisdom, who pours water—rendered as ankhs, symbols of life—over him. To the left, the king receives the breath of life from Horus, son of Osiris.

38

Ramps and steps leading to the sanctuary area rise from avenues of columns. By positioning the sanctuary at a higher level than the hypostyle halls, the builders were following a convention that called for the symbolic replication of the island of creation, site of the first temple.

WHERE ONLY KINGS AND PRIESTS COULD TREAD

As the home of the gods, Seti's temple would have been off-limits to all but pharaohs, officials, and priests, although ordinary folk may have been admitted to the forecourts on certain occasions. No part of it was more sacrosanct than the seven chapels to the rear and the chambers beyond, where the cult of Osiris was observed.

According to Egyptian belief, the gods dwelled in spirit within the chapels. To facilitate worship, however, they were represented there by statues. Treated as though they were flesh-and-blood individuals, the statues received daily care. Priests tended them in clouds of incense, bathed them, dressed them in fresh clothes, and presented them with food and drink.

Although Seti knew well that the dim light of the temple would make many of the scenes located on the high wall in front of the chapels difficult to see, he left no detail out, eager not so much to please the eyes of mortals as to gain the favor of the gods. Still bearing paint, the reliefs depict Seti performing all of the numerous aspects of his religious obligations, with hieroglyphs spelling out appropriate prayers and incantations.

The pharaoh's artists outlined the figures on a tight grid and then proceeded to carve them in the stone, generally in three-quarter profile. This standard approach reflected the Egyptian view of eternity: the perfection, and thus unchanging nature, of all things from the beginning of time.

Hidden behind a column (left) is the central chapel of the chief god, Amen. Statues of divinities probably stood in the niches to either side. The reliefs are considered among Egypt's most beautiful; the one above shows Iusas, partner of Atum, the creator god, bestowing the breath of life on Seti.

In the shrine of Isis, wife and sister of Osiris, Seti offers the goddess two bowls of wine. For the temple decorations, Seti used raised relief, more refined and more difficult to execute than the incised carving that was employed by Ramses following his father's death.

IN THE REALM OF SYMBOLS AND MAGIC

The walls of Seti's temple resonated with symbolic meaning. The scene pictured at right from the chapel of Osiris, for example, shows staffs carried in royal funeral processions, capped with gods associated with the afterlife. Here the deities are represented in animal form. Wepwawet, symbolizing both Upper and Lower Egypt, is seen twice as a canine. On the first standard, far to the left, he perches atop a serpent, an animal connected with eternity because of its skin-shedding habit. On the second standard, he reclines. At Abydos, emblems of Wepwawet would have led off the solemn processions for which the items in this panel are the paraphernalia. The paddlelike object beneath the second figure of Wepwawet is a *sekhem*, emblem of Anubis, the mortuary god. On the third pole stands Horus, followed by Onuri-Shu, a local god. The column dominating the scene is the reliquary of Osiris, which supposedly contained his head. It is anchored to a shrine that would have been carried through throngs of awe-struck worshipers.

At far left, a bowl of incense, "the sweat of the god, which fell to earth," pokes into the scene, imbuing it with purity. At far right, blue lotuses atop a table laden with jars of unguents express the Egyptian hope of regeneration after death.

A MONUMENTAL CELEBRATION OF SELF

Workers guide a 21-ton head of Ramses II into place during the relocation of one of the pharaoh's greatest accomplishments, his monument at Abu Simbel. The structure was rescued from submersion by waters of the Aswan High Dam, built to control the flow of the Nile.

Early in the 19th century, the renowned Swiss traveler and Arabist Johann Ludwig Burckhardt undertook a journey up the Nile River into the ancient land of Nubia. Far to the south of Aswan, his eye caught a colossal stone head protruding from the sand above the riverbank. Burckhardt looked up and marveled at the giant face: "A most expressive, youthful countenance," he wrote, "approaching nearer to the Grecian model of beauty than of any ancient Egyptian figure I have seen." What he had discovered, in fact, was the head of but one of four huge statues of the pharaoh Ramses II—the rest of them lay totally submerged under tons of windblown sand piled up over the centuries. Although Burckhardt had no way of knowing what lay hidden below, he wrote with remarkable prescience: "Could the sand be cleared away, a vast temple would be discovered."

A few years later in 1817, the Italian strongman, inventor, and amateur archaeologist Giovanni Belzoni, inspired by Burckhardt's descriptions, dug out that temple, known today by its local name, Abu Simbel. After 22 days of clearing away the sand in the scorching August heat, Belzoni and his crew finally gazed upon the fully revealed "four enormous sitting colossi, the largest in Egypt or Nubia, except the great Sphinx at the pyramids, to which they approach in the proportion of near two-thirds."

Further digging eventually disclosed a door set in the rockface between the statues. Excitedly, Belzoni's party stepped inside. The interior contained several chambers carved from solid rock, and Belzoni immediately perceived that it was "a very large place; but our astonishment increased, when we found it to be one of the most magnificent temples, enriched with beautiful intaglios [incised figures], painting, colossal figures, etc."

Belzoni tried making a record of some of the wondrous battle scenes that were carved in relief, but "the heat was so great that it scarcely permitted us to take any drawings, as the perspiration from our hands soon rendered the paper quite wet. Accordingly, we left this operation to succeeding travelers, who may set about it with more convenience than we could, as the place will become cooler." Since the deciphering of hieroglyphs was still some five years away, Belzoni could not know the identity of the man who had built this temple, whose image loomed everywhere, both inside and out. But

A turn-of-the-century photograph shows a gigantic statue of Ramses II lying on its back in a palm grove at the site of Memphis. The likeness was but one of 11 colossi that Ramses commissioned of himself to occupy commanding positions near the Temple of Ptah, patron god of artisans.

it was, in fact, not Giovanni Belzoni's first encounter with the glories of Egypt's most famous pharaoh.

The year before, Belzoni had seen another large stone bust on the western side of the Nile, across from Thebes, about 350 miles north of Abu Simbel. The statue had—erroneously—become known as "the young Memnon," lying outside the ruins of a temple that was assumed to be the Memnonium. Belzoni was stunned by the work: "I must say that my expectations were exceeded by its beauty," he later wrote, "but not by its size."

The statue had once been a complete figure, but, ravaged by vandalism, the elements, and earthquakes over the past three millennia, only the head and shoulders remained intact. Even so, the half-buried fragment weighed more than seven tons, and it took the Italian and his team of hired laborers 17 days to drag it to the nearby riverbank. He later described the implements he had brought with him from Cairo: "14 poles, 8 of which were employed in making a sort of car to lay the bust on, four ropes of palm leaves, and four rollers, without tackle of any sort."

Of the 80 workers Belzoni had requested from the local authorities, only a few showed up at the beginning, although later he would end up with 130. "By means of four levers," he wrote, "I raised the bust, so as to leave a vacancy under it to introduce the car; and after it was slowly lodged on this, I had the car raised in front so as to get one of the rollers underneath. I then had the same operation performed at the back. Lastly, I placed men in the front, distributing them equally at the four ropes."

On the first day, July 27, Belzoni managed to move the bust only several yards from its original site. On the next, he made 50 yards, deliberately breaking the bases of two columns at the temple to clear a path for his burden. After 150 yards, the statue unexpectedly sank in the sand, and a detour of more than 300 yards on firmer ground had to be sought. But the new course seemed to be a great improvement over the first, and progress steadily increased. Sick from constant exposure to the burning summer sun and interrupted by another no-show of his workers, Belzoni did not reach the Nile with his precious cargo until August 12. A boat then carried the bust downstream to Alexandria, for eventual transshipment to the British Museum in London, where it rests today.

Belzoni was justly proud of his efforts; previous treasure hunters had been unable to shift the enormous head at all. But considering that the broken bust comprised only a fraction of the original complete figure, his achievement pales in comparison to that of Ramses' workers, who had gouged the monolith out of bedrock, then carved and transported the entire statue from its distant quarry to Thebes.

As exploration of Egypt continued throughout the 19th century—and scholars could finally read the hieroglyphic inscriptions—more and more images of Ramses II were identified. On statues, temples, steles, and obelisks from the Nile Delta to Nubia, the king's signature, or his cartouche, reading "Usi-ma-re Setepenre" (Strong in Right is Re, Chosen of Re) seemed to be everywhere *(page 21)*. No ruler before or since—not even Ramses' idol, the great builder Amenhotep III—had such an obsessive interest in the proliferation of his own likeness.

And yet, for all that, Ramses was not so fundamentally different from either his predecessors or his successors as pharaoh. For Egypt's rulers were not just monarchs, raised above other mortals to be masters of the land. First and foremost, the pharaoh was the mediator between the gods and the people of the Nile, a role he had fulfilled since the earliest times. He was responsible for maintaining stability in the Egyptian universe, upholding justice, order, righteousness, and truth. These essential harmonies were grouped together in the concept of Maat, personified by the goddess of the same name, who was also the daughter of Re.

The pharaoh contributed to Maat in the first instance simply by existing. As king, he was considered the earthly embodiment of the falcon god Horus, and on his enthronement he acquired a name that reflected one of the god's attributes. Ramses' father had been "Strong Bull Appearing in Thebes" and "Nourishing the Two Lands"; Ramses chose to be "Strong Bull, Beloved of Right, Truth." Like so many of his predecessors, the pharaoh was also "Son of Re," under that god's special protection.

But over millennia, Egyptian theology had evolved an immense subtlety; it was the office of pharaoh that enacted the role of the god Horus and not the man who for a brief lifetime occupied the office. When the king died, however, his permanent transmutation to godhood was assured. His successor, the next embodiment of the

An artist took the liberty of restoring the missing face of Ramses II in this 1842 lithograph of the broken, seated colossus—the famed "Ozymandias"—that occupied the first court of the Ramesseum, the pharaoh's mortuary temple. In the photograph at right, columns frame the fragments, still lying where they fell when the sculpture was toppled by an earthquake.

god Horus, would lay him to rest, at which time he would join his dead ancestors in becoming one with Osiris and take his place with them in the Egyptian pantheon. The cult of the dead god-king would be observed forever in his specially built mortuary temple, "The Mansion of Millions of Years." Ceremonies there would include anointing and clothing the image of the god-pharaoh, as well as presenting it with freshly prepared food and drink daily, just as was done for other gods such as Amen, Ptah, and Re in their temples. On the correct performance of these rituals, so the Egyptians believed, the future of the nation hung.

In practical terms, however, a satisfactory state of Maat was the result of a pharaoh's daily actions. In theory at least, the pharaoh was the high priest of every temple, responsible for the religious observances of the entire nation. He was also the head of state, Egypt's civil ruler, its lawmaker, and its supreme judge. His buildings, columns, obelisks, steles, and statues, his construction of monuments in almost every town under his dominion announced clearly to the people that all was well with the world.

Ramses had already shown great interest in building materials and projects as prince regent. He had seen and admired the work on his father's magnificent tomb in the Valley of the Kings and the building of Seti's beautiful temple to Osiris at Abydos. And, like his father, he admired Amenhotep III's abundant, large-scale, and tasteful designs. The young Ramses can hardly be blamed for dreaming of following in Amenhotep's footsteps—perhaps even surpassing his achievements one day.

Although his father had permitted him to begin his own smaller temple to Osiris at Abydos, Ramses had to wait until he became pharaoh himself before launching his more ambitious plans. Unlike Seti, who had chosen finely drawn decorations in the low-relief style for his temples, Ramses preferred incised carvings, which could be done more quickly and were much harder to erase by any future king who might be tempted to usurp his work—a practice Ramses himself employed on numerous occasions when he recycled earlier pharaohs' efforts for his own gain.

When Seti I died, the people could already sense that Ramses would be one of Egypt's great builders. From the beginning, the new ruler contemplated construction projects on a vast scale. First there

A carved column depicts Ramses II with two symbols of rebirth and rejuvenation, the lotus flower and the falcon god Horus. The column, first inscribed and erected by Thutmose IV, was usurped by Ramses 100 to 150 years later, then recycled as building material by the Romans in the 1st century AD.

was Pi-Ramses—the expansion of Seti's summer palace and ancestral home at Avaris in the Nile Delta into an entirely new capital city. Meanwhile, Ramses had ordered some mighty works in the south: He took advantage of the voyage to Thebes in connection with his father's funeral not only to command the completion of Seti's mortuary temple but also to order the construction of his own massive tomb and to lay out personally the foundation of his grandiose mortuary temple, the Ramesseum.

Additionally, Ramses could not help but be drawn to the large temple complex at Karnak, opposite the Valley of the Kings, on the east bank of the Nile, which modern excavators believe had been continuously enlarged and restored over the two millennia in which it was in use. It eventually covered 60 acres and included 20 temples, shrines, and halls built and dedicated to different gods. At least 15 obelisks were erected there during the New Kingdom alone.

Ramses' father had commissioned a huge hypostyle hall, the largest hall of columns in the world, covering an area of some 54,000 square feet with a forest of 134 columns and a central roof almost 80 feet high. Ramses saw to the still unfinished hall's completion and changed its name to "Effective is Ramses II." The interior walls recorded his divine coronation and other sacred scenes for which he partially usurped the wall reliefs of his father, Seti. On the outside walls Ramses was later to put reliefs depicting his military campaigns in Canaan and Syria for all to see, including the battle of Kadesh and, nearby, a copy of the famous peace treaty with the Hittites.

At the main Amen temple in Karnak, Ramses would build a gateway on the eastern side, flanked by two colossal statues of himself, where ordinary people, not allowed into the inner sanctum, could leave petitions for the gods with their intermediary, the king. He also ordered the construction of a landing dock on the Nile, which was connected to the Karnak temple by an avenue that was

Amen's precinct at Karnak, seen below from the Sacred Lake where priests purified themselves before entering the temples, included numerous magnificent structures built over centuries. Silhouetted at dusk are huge pylons (at left and center), *and the obelisk of Queen Hatshepsut* (far right). *To the right of the central pylon looms Ramses II's hypostyle hall, portrayed in the early 19th-century reconstruction at right.*

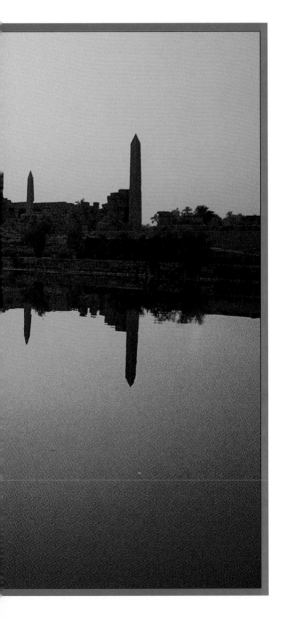

lined with 120 ram-headed sphinxes, all of them holding a small image of the king between their paws.

Two miles away at the Temple of Amen, which is known today as the Temple of Luxor, Ramses built a colonnaded court and pylon, for which plans had already been made. But on the walls and pylon towers the pharaoh later added still more reliefs and texts extolling Kadesh. He also had two enormous obelisks and six colossal statues of himself set at the temple's entrance. While one obelisk remains in situ, the second obelisk was removed by the French in the 1830s to commemorate Napoleon's troops, who took part in the expedition to Egypt in 1798-1799. It was reerected in the Place de la Concorde in Paris in the presence of some 200,000 spectators. There for all to see, but few to read, was the pharaoh's haughty inscription: "A ruler great in wrath, mighty in strength, every land trembles at him, because of his renown."

The young Ramses had been put in charge of the quarry at Aswan, located more than 150 miles upstream from Thebes and the source of most of Egypt's granite, as part of his grooming for the highest office in the land. He had also supervised the transport of what one of Seti's rock inscriptions described as "very great obelisks and great and marvelous statues."

There was such a voracious demand for permanent building material in ancient Egypt that hardly a rock formation could be found which was not used as a quarry. Since the time of the 18th Dynasty, most of the sandstone used in the buildings at Karnak had come from the huge quarries at Gebel Silsila, located about 100 miles south of Thebes. Ramses II—and later his successor, Ramses III—also used sandstone from this site in the construction of their mortuary temples across the Nile from Thebes.

Transport downstream from Gebel Silsila was not overly difficult, since ships could practically sail into the harborlike quarry bays on either side of the Nile. The sandstone blocks were loaded onto sledges and hauled along specially built ramps to the river. Some notations found at the Ramesseum show that 64 blocks in 10 ships could have arrived daily from Gebel Silsila, and an inscription from the quarry itself mentions that 3,000 men and 40 vessels were needed to produce and transport the stones for Ramses III's temple.

Unfinished sandstone sphinxes, such as the ones that line

Ramses II's processional road from the river landing to the temple at Karnak, still lie scattered about the quarries of Gebel Silsila. The columns of the hypostyle hall at Karnak were also sandstone and came from the same quarries.

All quarries in Egypt were owned by the pharaoh, and Ramses, more than most, took a hands-on approach. His youthful experience at Aswan seems to have convinced him he had a natural eye for a good piece of rock. Certainly, in his unceasing search for monumental grandeur, the king left no stone unturned—or rather, unhewn, if it was large enough. At Aswan, according to the inscription on a stele, he informed his sculptors that he had personally "examined a fine mountain in order that I might give you the use of it."

Taking a stroll in the desert near Heliopolis once, Ramses discovered a large deposit of very rare quartzite, "the like of which had never been found since the beginning of time," as a stele dating from the eighth year of his reign put it. Murderously hard to work, it was a material highly prized for its immense durability, and Ramses at once ordered his sculptors to make use of this block, which was "higher than a granite obelisk." According to the stele, they chiseled it into a gigantic statue of the king, later erected in Pi-Ramses. Unfortunately, no trace of it has ever been found.

Other Ramses colossi, though, are less elusive. For the Ramesseum, which in most respects follows the pattern for mortuary temples established by Ramses' predecessors, the king decided to add a unique feature. The entrance courtyard would be dominated by a gigantic seated statue of himself, 66 feet high. (This, the largest surviving colossus he ever commissioned, is the shattered "Ozymandias"—Shelley's inspiration—which still lies at the Ramesseum.) Even for Egypt's engineers and sculptors, heirs to some 1,500 years of massive stone construction, the prospect was daunting. Weighing about a thousand tons, it would be the largest known statue ever carved from a single piece of granite.

The main source of the stone during Ramses' day was Aswan. Although no trace remains there of the quarrying of the Ramesseum colossus, an unfinished obelisk of an even larger size—138 feet long, which could have weighed 1,200 tons at completion—gives a clear picture of the methods that must have been utilized, having been abandoned when ill luck or carelessness left the monument fatally cracked. As a first step, the stone had to be cut from the living rock. Egyptian technology offered no shortcuts for that task; the bronze

On a barren, isolated plateau in the Sinai, a few upright steles stand amid the rubble of the Temple of Hathor, patron goddess of miners, at Serabit el Khadim. For hundreds of years, Egypt's pharaohs sent expeditions here to work nearby turquoise mines and bring back the highly prized semiprecious stone.

and copper tools produced by the pharaoh's smiths were far too soft to make any impression on granite, and the job was done by human muscle pounding stone on stone.

First, overseers marked an outline on the quarry floor. Then, gangs of laborers chipped narrow trenches around at least three sides of the monument-to-be with 10-pound balls of dolerite, a basaltic rock even harder than granite itself. Each blow removed only a few flakes; but as the weeks and months went by, the trenches slowly deepened to the required depth. Meanwhile, on the fourth side, other workers hewed an open pathway clear out of the quarry, while their companions undercut the block, probably the most difficult part of the quarrying. Squatting below ground level in a stone trench no more than 30 inches wide, they had to extricate the whole piece from the bedrock, pounding away at its foundation and using a series of huge wooden levers to break it free.

This assignment—carried out on sweltering sunbaked stone in temperatures that could reach 140° Fahrenheit—was enervating to the work force, a mixture of conscripted peasant labor, slaves, prisoners of war, and criminals, guilty of offenses serious enough to have them "sent to the granite." The peasants toiled in the quarries only from July through September, when the annual inundation of the Nile made their fields unworkable. In return, the government would provide them with subsistence during the time of year when they would otherwise have no source of income.

As for the other categories of laborers, they could not look forward to any respite; a pair of carved steles at Abu Simbel, representing the life story of Setau, viceroy of Nubia during much of Ramses' reign, list some of his accomplishments—"I directed serfs in thousands and ten-thousands, and Nubians in hundred-thousands, without limit." On another stele, an army officer named Ramose describes how, in 1247 BC, "His Majesty commanded the confidant, the Viceroy of Nubia, Setau, together with army personnel of the company of Ramses II that he should take captives from the land of the Libyans, in order to build in the Temple of Ramses II."

Unskilled workers were not the quarries' only employees; some of Egypt's best sculptors were based there as well. It was for these skilled workers that Ramses himself had played prospector, and whom he exhorted jovially: "You chosen workmen, valiant men of proven skill, craftsmen in valuable stone, experienced in granite, familiar with quartzite, good fellows tireless and vigilant at work all day. I am your constant provider. I know your labors to be eager and

A 138-foot-long unfinished obelisk at an Aswan granite quarry demonstrates how large blocks of stone were extracted from bedrock. Laborers painstakingly pounded rock on rock to form trenches around and under the block, then roughly dressed the granite to its desired shape. Work on the monument stopped more than 3,000 years ago when cracks developed, precluding its removal.

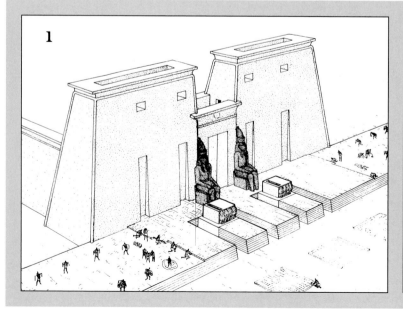

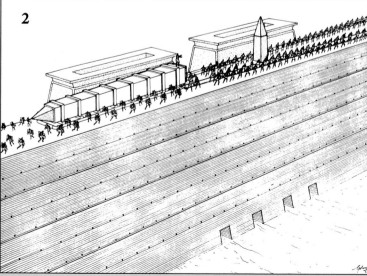

able, and that work is [only] a pleasure with a full stomach. The granaries groan with grain for you. None of you [need] pass the night moaning about poverty."

These elite and clearly well-paid stoneworkers began their carving on the next obelisk or future colossus even as the rough-hewn block slowly emerged from bedrock. Often all but the finest details of a piece were completed at the quarry, for the more they cut away, the easier the sculpture would be to move. For the transportation of obelisks, ramps were built from the quarry to the riverbank, where giant barges pulled by rowboats delivered the monuments to their destination and another waiting ramp.

No contemporary description has survived to explain how these heavy, unwieldy blocks were loaded onto the barges in Ramses' day. But an account by the Roman Pliny the Elder, written in the 1st century AD, details an ingenious system from the Ptolemaic era, almost 1,000 years after Ramses' death, that would have been well within the abilities of his engineers. To float a huge obelisk, workers would first drag it across a canal, forming a kind of temporary bridge. Then they would position barges, heavily ballasted with stones, underneath it. When the ballast was removed, the barges rose in the water to take the weight of the obelisk and carry it downstream, where, presumably, the same procedure was reversed.

The most complicated part of the procedure must have been the last phase—erecting the obelisk at the site. This assumption seems

The sketches below illustrate one theory of how Egyptian engineers raised obelisks, a difficult feat even in modern times. From left to right, with the bases for two of the monuments in place (1), workers mold mud bricks and begin building a huge temporary structure that will have ramps at either end. Having dragged one obelisk up such a slope and set it in place, workers draw the second across the top of the structure to a wide-mouthed shaft filled partially with sand (2). Once they have positioned the obelisk in the shaft, they start removing the sand (3), which permits the obelisk to descend slowly until it makes contact with the base. Finally, they pull the monument upright with ropes (4). One scholar estimated that 2,000 men would have been required to position the 227-ton obelisk still in front of the Temple of Luxor.

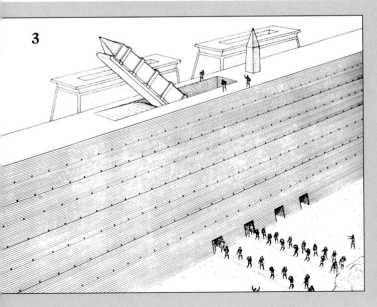
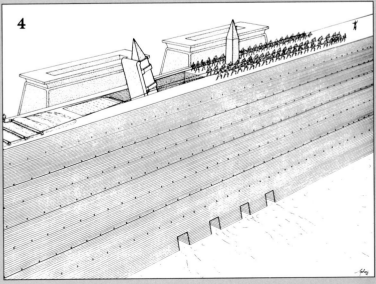

to be supported by the fact that not one Egyptian obelisk was ever precisely installed; although they stand vertically, all of them show a slight axial deviation relative to the base. Suggested theories on how an obelisk was raised highlight the difficulties that were involved. The workers would first haul the monolith up an inclined ramp to a raised, level earthen platform. They would then move it to the edge of a hole dug down through the platform to the foundation stone, upon which the obelisk would stand, and begin to edge the obelisk in. One can imagine the precarious moment when the giant stone column began to tip upwards and slide into the hole, people furiously tugging on ropes to keep it from moving too quickly and shattering upon impact with the base *(pages 56-57)*. It would certainly require the utmost concentration. Pliny the Elder wrote—perhaps apocryphally—that the pharaoh whom he called Rhamesis demanded that one of his own sons be tied to the tip of the obelisk to ensure the fullest attention from the workers.

From paintings and reliefs in tombs and temples, it is known that colossal statues were secured to sledges and dragged by a huge labor force over a track that was lubricated with Nile mud or water. The two huge quartzite statues of Amenhotep III, known as the Colossi of Memnon and weighing some 700 tons each, had to be transported overland in this manner from the quarry at Gebel Ahmar, east of modern Cairo, to western Thebes—a distance of almost

A drawing of a 12th-Dynasty tomb painting depicts a worker standing on the base of a stone colossus pouring water on the ground to create a slick surface. This done, the 172 men will begin dragging the sledge on which the figure sits. Since the statue probably weighed 58 tons, each man would have had to contribute 675 pounds of pulling power to slide it forward. An early 20th-century engineer found that under similar conditions a single man could move one ton.

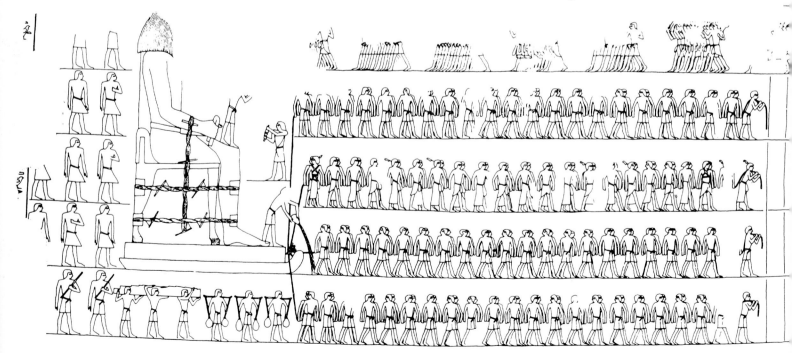

500 miles. Using the Nile was out of the question in this particular case; no boat could possibly have hauled such a massive load upstream against the river's current.

Fortunately for Ramses and his work crews, the Ramesseum lies downstream from the quarry at Aswan and "Ozymandias" could be floated most of the way. In fact, the workers could even spare themselves most of the arduous three-mile overland trip from the riverbank by timing the transport to coincide with the Nile's inundation and bringing the statue right to the temple's doorstep. (Traces of a landing dock have been found near the ruins.)

Once in the temple precinct, only the third and last problem remained to be solved—the statue's final erection. Just how this was accomplished remains a matter of conjecture, but according to modern calculations, either 200 oxen or 1,000 men would have been required to move the 1,000-ton monolith. Perhaps some form of ramp or inclined plane was involved, up which the statue was dragged until it could slide over onto its foundation. And another image of the king—his features carved to reflect eternity—could look serenely down upon his people.

During the reign of Ramses II, such high visibility undertakings formed only part of the total effort devoted to construction. Some projects, on the other hand, were never meant to be seen by the public, such as the Valley of the Kings, where, as tradition required, work had begun on the pharaoh's tomb as soon as he was crowned. Almost three centuries before Ramses' birth, his great predecessor Thutmose I had started the custom of burial here, attracted by the valley's empty silence—not to mention its distance from any settlement that might conceal a band of tomb robbers.

Of course, the isolation created logistical problems for the construction teams. So, in an adjoining valley about a mile from the edge of the Nile's green belt and concealed from populated areas by a low hill, Thutmose I created a permanent settlement—now called Deir el Medina—for the artisans who would build, decorate, and furnish not only his own tomb but also those of most of his successors, their nobles, and high officials.

The village was clearly useful, and the kings who followed Thutmose continued to maintain it. From about 1500 to 1100 BC, the inhabitants of the village—who were known variously as the

"Workmen of the Royal Tomb" and "Servants of the Place of Truth"—formed a thriving community.

These laborers and their families were in a very different category from the unskilled workers at Aswan and elsewhere who toiled in the construction of Egypt's public monuments. Indeed, the term *workmen* may be somewhat misleading; many were clearly highly skilled professionals, including artists well respected by their royal employer and his ministers. "The Governor and Vizier Paser has sent to me saying 'let the dues be brought for the workmen of the Royal Tomb,' " wrote the mayor of western Thebes, " 'namely vegetables, fish, firewood, jars of beer, victuals and milk. Do not let a scrap of it remain outstanding.' " Other records assess the annual salary of a skilled man as 48 *khar* of emmer wheat—about 100 bushels—four times what the village's porters were paid.

A police detachment manned checkpoints at the entrances to the area, largely to keep outsiders out. Fear of tomb robbers was, of course, one reason why Thutmose had begun the development of the Valley of the Kings in the first place, and stringent efforts were made to preserve secrecy and security. And though the work the inhabitants of Deir el Medina executed in the royal tombs obeyed the conventions of Egyptian funeral art, the artists were not above a little satirical sketching in their own time: Some of the ostraca found there show idle, aristocratic mice waited on by servile, long-suffering cats.

The workers knew how to enjoy their free time—especially if it coincided with the feast of the village's patron, the deified Amenhotep I. Thus on Day 29 of the Third Month of Winter, or so a fragment records, "the gang made merry before him for four full days, drinking with their wives and children—60 people from inside [the village] and 60 people from outside services."

The great trove of scribbled ostraca from Deir el Medina has yielded fascinating examples of how everyday commerce was managed in Egypt's cashless civilization. Although there was nothing resembling a formal coinage, even as late as the end of the New Kingdom, a highly standardized barter system, in which almost everything had an agreed equivalent in metal or grain, came close to providing the flexibility of a money economy. Thus, in one purchase listed on an ostracon from Deir el Medina, a coffin was reckoned to be worth 25½ *deben* of copper; at a little over three ounces per deben, that came to about five pounds of metal.

However, the buyer did not simply offer copper in exchange.

His upturned hands signifying reverence—and fleshy body showing the signs of both age and prosperity—May, Ramses II's architect, personifies the successful public servant. Following in his father's footsteps as chief of works, May erected temples and state buildings in Egypt's major cities.

Instead, he tendered a hog valued at 5 deben, two goats at 5 deben for the pair, two sycamore logs worth a deben apiece, and, to make up the difference, two separate weighings from his hoard of actual copper, which amounted to 13½ deben. In another deal, a village policeman bought from a workman an ox for the equivalent of 50 deben. The officer had only 5 deben in metal, so he made up the balance with a jar of fat (presumably a large one, since it was considered equal to 30 copper deben), two tunics worth 10 deben, and 5 deben's worth of vegetable oil.

The villagers' labor had a regular routine: an eight-hour shift daily through a 10-day "week," with the 10th day set aside for rest and the issue of rations. The unprecedented duration of Ramses' reign during the New Kingdom, however, had a downside for the village; with no turnover at the top, the demand for royal tombs fell off. By Ramses' 40th year on the throne, some of the workers averaged only one day of work out of four and could devote time to preparations for their own afterlife: They carved tombs for themselves into a hillside above the little community.

There were some limits to Ramses'—or any pharaoh's—power, created not by any organized opposition so much as the sheer complexity of the pharaonic state. To a degree the only pillar of Egyptian society that might be said to have been beyond the pharaoh's immediate control was the network of temples and the priestly hierarchies who served them. From a distance of 3,000 years, these may appear to be even more important than they were, based solely on the archaeological remains that are scattered around Egypt.

A right angle and plumb bob was as much a tool of the builder's trade in Ramses' time as it is today. This instrument, discovered in an overseer's tomb near Thebes, is inscribed with a plea for a long life and a good burial from his patron, the god Ptah.

Royal palaces were constructed mainly from mud brick, and the years have largely erased them. But during the New Kingdom, monumental temples built mostly of stone arose, which, after the pyramids, became the country's most enduring architectural legacy. And in contrast to earlier times, these larger, New Kingdom stone temples began to appear in the heart of Egyptian communities, meaning ordinary Egyptians could now experience buildings on a monumental scale at the center of their daily lives.

Yet the more visible proximity of the great temples to the people did not bring the people any closer to what lay within: Nei-

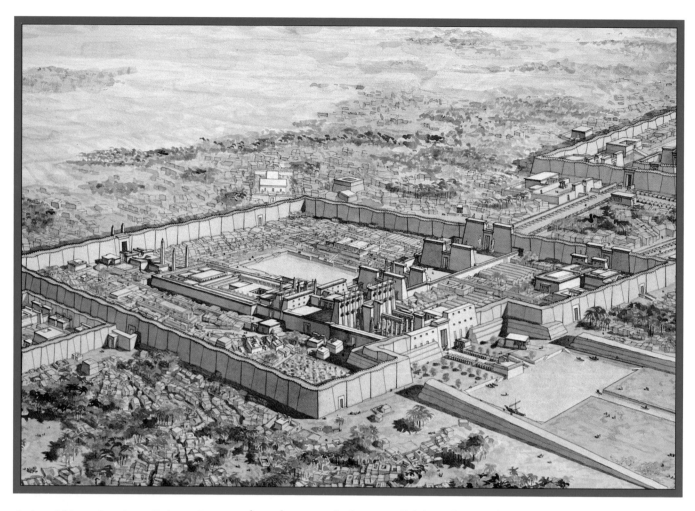

A city within a city, the walled temple complex at Karnak evolved over 20 centuries, growing from a modest shrine to 60 acres of monuments. The continual additions and alterations by successive pharaohs, each trying to outdo the others, signaled the increasing power of religion and the priesthood in Egypt.

ther the temples' powerful interior architecture nor their exquisite adornment were ever intended to impress ordinary human eyes. Temple religion in Egypt had never involved public participation —except for the feast days.

The New Kingdom era placed a much greater importance on these religious parades and public festivals, at which portable images of the gods were taken from their shrines and carried in a sacred boat—but still hidden within veiled cabins—from one temple to another or along a processional way to the riverbank *(page 67)*. Some of these ceremonies were seasonal ones, celebrating the arrival of spring or of a new year. Others were closely related to a particular god, like the Opet festival of Amen that Ramses had attended not long after his coronation.

These processions were immensely popular occasions, and with good reason. They were holidays in which food and beer were liberally dispensed from temple stocks. They not only brought color into the drab workaday lives of the peasantry but also demonstrated, through royal generosity, that the country's relationship with its gods remained in reliable hands—especially if the pharaoh himself was in attendance.

The well-being and, indeed, the very survival of the nation depended on the continued goodwill of the gods, which could only be assured by careful attention to ritual. Worship of the main gods, such as Amen, Re, and Ptah, was far too serious a matter to be performed other than in private. All that common Egyptians ever saw of their society's most pervasive institutions was the inscrutable blankness of the outer mud-brick temple walls that concealed their mysteries, although on rare occasions some individuals might be admitted into the forecourts. One outstanding exception was the hypostyle hall at Karnak, which Ramses ordered to be opened to the public. He called it "The Place Where the Common People Extol the Name of His Majesty." Here the public could worship the gods and most of all "His Majesty," Ramses II.

But in most cases the walls were formidable barriers. Traces of

A two-mile-long avenue flanked by stone sphinxes led from Karnak to the Temple of Luxor (below), which, compared with Karnak's more complicated layout, exhibited an integrated and coherent design. The temple was built principally by two pharaohs, Amenhotep III and Ramses II.

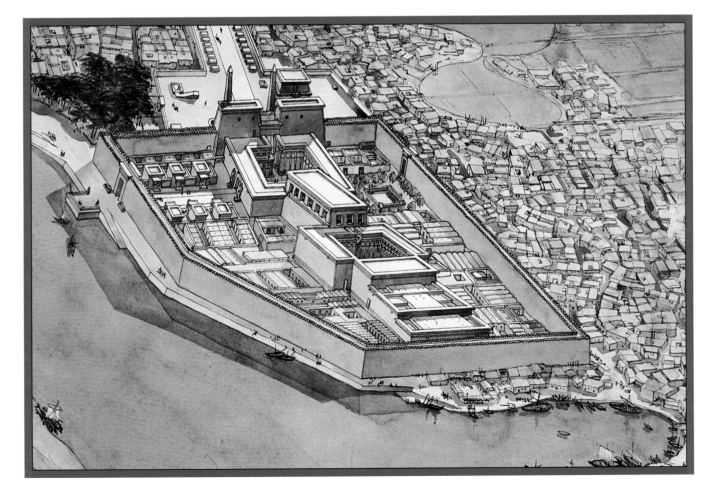

A RACE AGAINST TIME: PAINSTAKING EFFORTS TO RECORD A THREATENED LEGACY

Egypt's beloved monuments have long suffered the vicissitudes of time, but never have they been under more direct threat of destruction than they are today as throngs of tourists, pollution, a higher water table, and overcrowding by a burgeoning population begin to have an ever-increasing effect on them.

The gradual deterioration of the monuments has been evident for more than a century. In the 1920s James H. Breasted of the Oriental Institute of the University of Chicago decreed that "the supreme obligation of the present generation of Orientalists is to make a comprehensive effort to save for posterity the enormous body of ancient records surviving in Egypt." Thus it was with considerable urgency that the institute's Epigraphic Survey tackled the job of recording inscriptions and decorations on Egypt's monuments.

Among the greatest of these is the Temple of Luxor. The survey's goal is to provide "documentation so precise that it could stand alone as a replacement in the absence of the original monument." Accordingly, team members have spent innumerable hours copying the hieroglyphs and scenes on the walls of the temple, as well as fragments associated with it.

The Epigraphic Survey uses an exacting method to ensure accuracy. First a section of a relief is photographed; then the image is enlarged. An artist pencils all details of the original work directly onto the photograph. Next, the penciled lines are inked in and the picture is bleached, leaving only the artist's lines. The drawing is corrected at the temple wall by two Egyptologists, working independently, to ensure the accuracy of the hieroglyphs and the accompanying scenes. After the artist has made all of the necessary changes, the drawing is published, along with others made at the site, in a folio—part of the growing record on paper of the glory that once was Egypt's on stone.

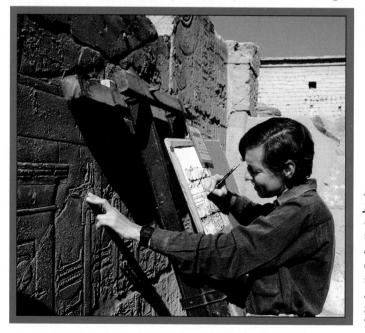

Perched on a ladder, with fingers touching a relief dating from Tutankhamen's time, an Epigraphic Survey artist pencils details onto a photographic blow-up of the carving. The relief is part of a series in the colonnade hall of the Temple of Luxor.

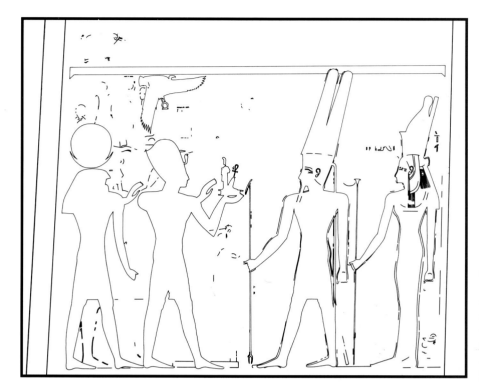

Four figures, outlined in this schematic drawing of a relief from the Temple of Luxor, were carved during Ramses II's reign. But traces of a relief belonging to the reign of the pharaoh Ay can also be made out, indicating that Ramses recarved the earlier work, superimposing his own.

From the surviving welter of faint lines on the wall usurped by Ramses, the Epigraphic Survey has been able to reconstruct the original scene, which shows Ay offering incense and libations to Amen and his wife, Mut.

an 18th-Dynasty wall, excavated at Karnak, indicate a forbidding, fortresslike structure, with square towers set into it at regular intervals. Ironically, the outer walls have proved more fragile than the stones they were built to protect, and modern-day tourists to Luxor or Karnak now see far more of the temples than all but a handful of people did in Ramses' time.

Ordinary Egyptians performed their devotions at local shrines—every province had its own indigenous, mostly animal-headed, gods—or sometimes as near to the great temples as they could. "Praise to thee at the great rampart," said an inscription on the wall of the Temple of Ptah in Memphis. "It is the place where prayer is heard." To emphasize that this was the spot where the gods were listening, large stone ears were positioned at the top of each tower of the walled enclosure.

Out of the sight of profane eyes, the temple could fulfill its one, overriding purpose, expressed more in being than in doing; the temple was *hwt-ntr,* nothing less than the "Mansion of the God." At its core, literally and symbolically, was the god's sanctuary, where in cultic gloom a sacred statue received the ritual service offered daily by a few select initiates.

In theory, only the pharaoh, because of his divine status, could represent his people before the gods, whether at a public festival or in the private oblations of the temple sanctuary. But, as a practical matter, he could not attend every function, and in his absence, one of the high priests substituted.

There were distinct rankings within the Egyptian priesthood: At the top, the high priests, or "first prophets," were frequently former high state officials, sometimes of royal blood themselves, and chosen more on account of their loyalty than any spiritual training. The next echelon included the second, third, and fourth prophets, "God's fathers"—scholars who were responsible for the more arcane aspects of theology and ritual.

But the great majority of those whose names are recorded with a priestly title appear to have been temple employees who performed a thrice-yearly stint of duties but in their lesser role were denied access to the sanctuary, the holy of holies. Before they were able to return to their regular outside professions, these lay priests had to be specially purified.

Besides rituals and ceremonies, much of the work in the temples was administrative—running and overseeing the gods' estates.

FESTIVALS FOR THE GODS THAT CHEERED THE HEART AND FILLED THE BELLY

The Egyptians loved life, and their religious festivals demonstrated it. During the Beautiful Feast of the Valley, the god Amen was brought from Karnak—in the form of a shrouded effigy carried on a golden bark *(below)*—and transported across the Nile to the west bank, Thebes's necropolis. There, on his annual one-day visit, Amen supposedly gave life to the dead. All along the processional route people turned out to greet him. In the evening the well-to-do crossed the river and feasted into the morning hours at the tombs of their ancestors, while the poor of Thebes and the surrounding countryside held their own celebrations. One hymn to Amen tells how they stayed awake "in the beauty of the night," the god's name echoing over their rooftops, as they sang his praises. Drinking was encouraged; indeed, drunkenness was seen as a way of dissolving the barriers between the living and the dead.

The Opet festival was also an occasion for merriment. It traditionally began when effigies of Mut and Khons, wife and son of Amen, joined the figure of Amen in his temple at Karnak. After being put aboard a gilded river barge, the three were towed to the Temple of Luxor. The gods resided there for three weeks, during which Amen performed oracularly and the divinity of kingship was reaffirmed. The journeys to and from the temples drew singers and musicians, as well as ordinary folk, happily getting drunk. "The whole land is in festivity," rejoices an Opet song. Just how relaxed an event it was is suggested by the beneficence of priests at Ramses II's mortuary temple, who are known to have handed out free 385 jugs of beer and 11,400 cakes and loaves of bread during one Opet.

And there was plenty of business to attend to; beyond religion, the temples had an economic function, too, and an important one. First and foremost, they were extremely rich. Royal endowments had made them major landowners in their own right—temple barges regularly cruised the Nile on rent-collecting missions. Additionally, the temples administered large tracts of the king's personal estates and, after every successful military campaign, received war booty as an offering to the gods in thanks for victory.

Royal largess often extended further. Ramses II gave his father's temple at Abydos a seagoing ship complete with crew. And both Abydos and Karnak were granted rights to desert gold mines, along with workers to bring the gold back. All major temples had their own merchant ships and traders, whose job it was to exchange surplus goods for temple necessities not in stock, and who appear to have had commercial links outside Egypt's borders.

Temples not only managed and engendered wealth; they also stockpiled it. The storerooms of the Ramesseum, for example, could accommodate enough grain to feed up to 20,000 people for a year. Such vast reserves obviously provided a safeguard against famine, but they also represented capital that could be used to finance major projects. In effect, the temples were probably the nearest thing that Egypt had to a banking system.

Wealth and power are usually inseparable, and the Egyptian temples were no exception. Certainly, they were subservient to the king, but they were also indispensable to him. There was a good deal of overlap between the priesthood and the royal bureaucracy, and the sheer quantity of administration handled by temple staff—they were frequently responsible for paying construction workers, for example—makes it hard to separate them from the regular machinery of state.

The clique of high-ranking priests was the only

68

An aerial view of the Ramesseum (above), reveals the enormous area surrounding the mortuary temple devoted to mud-brick vaults that once housed stores of grain. It would have taken 350 river barges such as the one at left, each loaded with 650 sacks of grain, to fill the Ramesseum's granary.

group with enough clout to challenge a pharaoh's incontestable will. Even Ramses had to go beyond Aswan or north to the delta, where the writ of the Upper Egyptian temple hierarchy did not run, to portray himself not just as the intermediary between the gods and humans but on equal footing with the gods. At Abu Simbel and elsewhere in Nubia he could proclaim his divine status—in life as well as death—without upsetting the priesthood. But Ramses' building projects and self-deification far up the Nile had a political basis, too, for the pharaohs were intent on impressing the Nubian population with their awesome powers.

Nubia, with its wealth of gold, had been the target of Egypt's kings since the days of the First Dynasty around 3,000 BC. By the end of the Middle Kingdom, Egyptian forts and fortified towns had risen at intervals along a stretch of some 300 miles from the first to the second cataract. In the New Kingdom, Egypt's empire reached

INGENIOUS SCHEMES FOR SAVING RAMSES' GREATEST MONUMENT FROM DROWNING

One of the 20th century's most extraordinary engineering feats, the rescue of Ramses II's Abu Simbel from the rising waters of the Aswan High Dam's reservoir, Lake Nasser, rivaled the pharaoh's own scheme for carving the monuments out of sandstone cliffs facing the Nile. The challenge was an enormous one: Relocate on higher ground the colossal figures of Ramses seated out front, the recessed temple behind them, and the statues of Ramses and his wife Nefertari standing close by, along with the queen's own temple, which was dug, like the pharaoh's, into the rock.

The operation to save the monument took over four years, cost nearly $40 million, and involved an international team of experts, as well as a small army of Egyptian laborers. All told some 3,000 people worked on the site between 1964 and 1968. Their presence in the desert required the building of housing, water lines, roads, airfields, docks, and communication networks, no mean feat in itself.

Teams first removed hundreds of thousands of tons of solid rock from behind the temples, then sawed the colossal figures and temples into 1,050 marked blocks weighing up to 33 tons each. After laying cement foundations, workers reassembled the blocks by fitting them with steel anchor bars and embedding them in reinforced concrete walls *(below)*.

Lest the saw marks show after the reassembly, workers inserted some 16 miles of sandstone-colored mortar into the joints between the stones.

For a while, it seemed that the rising waters of the reservoir might yet submerge the complex. In a race against the clock, a cofferdam was built to protect "against a man-made deluge," as an observer noted. Later the engineers of the Aswan High Dam decided to raise the level of the lake by 3.28 feet, thus obliging the Abu Simbel engineers to tear down their already partially finished reconstruction of Nefertari's temple and relocate it on still higher ground. Thus the temple, which once stood 12½ feet below Ramses' monument, is now but 6 feet lower.

This plan was only one of several submitted by countries around the world. The Italians wanted to cut the monument from the cliffs, enclose it in a reinforced concrete box, raise the whole structure on 650 synchronized jacks, and let it rest temporarily on prefabricated concrete pillars, repeating the

cycle until it reached high ground. The Americans suggested that the temples be cut free, floated on pontoons that would rise as the water level rose, and then transferred to dry ground. The French proposed constructing a 230-foot-high, mile-long dam around Abu Simbel to keep the water out.

Yet another proposal suggested that the monument should be allowed to drown and subsequently be viewed by visitors through glass corridors with the aid of floodlights. This scheme called for a thin membrane dam to filter out mud, equalize water pressure, and, through the introduction of beneficial chemicals, allow the porous sandstone to harden, preventing its decomposition. Not only were there to have been elevators and restaurants in this archaeological aquarium but also an artificial rising and setting sun.

It was the Swedish proposal to cut the monument into blocks and reassemble it some 200 feet higher that UNESCO, the sponsor of the project, decided to adopt. Today, the 3,200-year-old colossi continue to present their awesome appearance to the world. Yet behind them, hidden under pieces of fitted stone, is a concrete dome, 90 feet high with a 195-foot span, containing a modern lighting system and pumps that circulate fresh air through the two temples. Ramses would have been impressed.

still further, almost to the fifth cataract. This vast area, which extended some 800 miles up the Nile from Aswan, was the king's richest source of gold and slave labor.

But Nubia was by no means the most loyal of the pharaoh's provinces. Its population had always sat uneasily under Egyptian dominion, and uprisings occurred regularly. In 1294 BC, four years before Ramses' accession, the mere rumor of a planned rebellion in the relatively fertile Irem district beyond the Nile's third cataract had provoked Seti I into ordering a vigorous preemptive strike. As the viceroy of Nubia recorded, "Then said His Majesty to the high officers, courtiers and retinue, 'What are the despicable Irem, that they should dare transgress in My Majesty's time?' Then His Majesty dispatched the infantry and also much chariotry." If the inscription can be believed, the campaign was a whirlwind triumph: "The strong arm of Pharaoh was before them like a blast of fire, trampling the mountains," and within seven days all of the would-be rebels were either dead or captive.

A generation later, Ramses himself sent troops to help the viceroy of Nubia's own forces in another campaign against the Irem. While preferring to overawe his Nubian subjects through vast building projects and royal cults, Ramses did not hesitate to send in his forces against open dissidents. And if there was one thing that Ramses clearly enjoyed, it was overawing his subjects.

Of all Ramses' numerous monuments, none is more ostentatious than the rock-cut temple of Abu Simbel, located deep in Nubian territory. The king appears to have decided on the project during the first decade of his reign, when he saw two rose-colored sandstone cliffs towering above the Nile's west bank. As a method of showing the flag to some of Ramses' more troublesome subjects, the Abu Simbel temple complex served admirably. And far away from the priesthood of Egypt proper, there was nothing to restrain the pharaoh in his choice of imagery.

The main temple, whose original function was to honor the great gods of Egypt and Nubia, became the center of Ramses' personal cult in Nubia. It had a frontage composed of four seated statues of the pharaoh, carved from the living rock, each over 66 feet high; behind the huge figures, the halls and chambers of the temple were tunneled 160 feet into the cliff. Nearby, the second bluff was hewn into a subsidiary temple dedicated to the goddess Hathor. There, the facade consisted of four standing statues of Ramses and two of

Nefertari, the chief among his queens, flanked by smaller images of princes and princesses. According to the inscription that surrounds them, the temple had been cut as a tribute to Nefertari, "for whose sake the very sun does shine."

In case Abu Simbel was not enough, the king ordered other temples to be built in strategic areas of Nubia and made sure that he was enshrined as a resident deity in the temple of every major town; even the ornamental sphinxes that lined sacred avenues would bear Ramses' likeness. As prestige politics, his saturation campaign of self-aggrandizement was successful: There was no more trouble from the Nubians during Ramses' reign.

With the slow waning of Egyptian power after the end of the New Kingdom, the great rock carvings at Abu Simbel were eventually submerged by the relentless desert. When Belzoni and his workers cleared the sand away in 1817, they were the first people to look upon the temple in more than a thousand years. Now millions are familiar with the "expressive, youthful countenance" of Ramses II and have wondered what sort of a person would create such a titanic monument to himself.

The facile answer would be that the pharaoh had an enormous ego. Yet there was more to Ramses than the simple human foible of vanity. Perhaps he was indeed a megalomaniac; if so it was an occupational hazard to which every pharaoh—as undisputed, absolute ruler of the most powerful state in the world—was susceptible. There was far more to Ramses' ceaseless building and boasting than egotism; in part, at least, the king was doing no more than his duty. And plainly he believed in eternity.

A PHARAOH LARGER THAN LIFE

More than most leaders of great nations throughout history, Ramses II was all things to all people. War hero, conqueror, and peacemaker in his worldly role as pharaoh, he also fulfilled the country's spiritual needs in his role of intermediary between his subjects and the gods. In fact, over the course of his six and a half decades of absolute rule, he increasingly portrayed himself as a peer of the gods.

Ramses incorporated these many facets of his persona in the most enduring legacy of his lengthy reign—a prodigious construction program of palaces, temples, and statuary that spread his name, his image, and his exploits from the Nile Delta to the upper reaches of Nubia. Sometimes Ramses' message is blatantly propagandistic, as in the numerous wall reliefs and hieroglyphic descriptions of his "decisive" victory at Kadesh. In other cases the pharaoh displays an attitude of unpretentious piety; the dedication inscription of the Great Court of Ramses II at the Temple of Luxor

(above) describes it as a "monument for his father, Amen-Re, king of gods, of fine white sandstone, which the Son of Re, Ramses, made for him."

Other sites, such as Abu Simbel, served a dual purpose: The four astoundingly massive figures of Ramses provided an emphatic reminder of the pharaoh's control over the frequently troublesome region of Nubia, while inside, in the sanctuary of the temple, a smaller statue of the pharaoh received equal play with the gods Ptah, Amen, and Re.

Like everything else that archaeologists have learned about the man, Ramses' building projects bespeak vigor and might on a herculean scale. Even in a ruined state, the stone temples, statues, and obelisks—the mud-brick residences have long since crumbled to dust—have inspired awe since the first tourists cruised the Nile in Greek and Roman times. To the modern world, Ramses II is almost synonymous with the glories of ancient Egypt.

Two badly damaged statues of Ramses flank the entrance to his colonnaded Great Court at the Temple of Luxor. The pharaoh's ubiquitous cartouche can still be seen on the colossus at left. In the left foreground stands the 82-foot-high obelisk also shown on the previous page. Its mate, whose base is seen at right, now graces Paris's Place de la Concorde.

The soaring columns of Karnak's hypostyle hall—started by Seti I, Ramses' father—represent a papyrus thicket, symbolizing the watery, primeval landscape where creation occurred. Ramses thought nothing of usurping some of the reliefs that his father had commissioned and having them recarved in his own name.

A row of ram-headed sphinxes, emblem of the chief deity, Amen, once formed part of the processional avenue that ran from the Nile quay to the god's temple at Karnak. They were moved to their present location in the temple's first court after Ramses' death. Each sandstone animal holds a small figure, thought to be that of the pharaoh, between its paws.

The ruined yet still majestic shell of the Ramesseum rises from the desert's edge across the river from Thebes. The four pillars portray Ramses as the embodiment of the god Osiris. The heads may have broken off during the same earthquake that toppled the nearby "Ozymandias" statue.

The sun's early morning rays enhance the inherently reddish tinge of Ramses' masterpiece, the sandstone temple at Abu Simbel. Now safely ensconced above the waters of Lake Nasser, the pharaoh's visage may continue to gaze out upon a much-changed world for millennia yet to come.

Eight figures of Ramses, again representing Osiris, guard the corridor leading to Abu Simbel's deepest recesses. Twice a year sunlight penetrates the full 160 feet into the temple to shine directly on the pharaoh's face (below). Only Ramses and the priests could enter this chamber.

OF QUEENS, CONSORTS, AND COMMONERS

Late in the autumn of the year 1257 BC, a great caravan, attended by formations of armed soldiers and charioteers and bearing a dazzling array of gifts and treasures, wended its way out of the rugged uplands of Anatolia. Marching south into Syria, the procession paused at the boundary between the two mightiest empires of the age, where the domain of Hattusilis III, great king of the Hittites, bordered the realm of Ramses II, pharaoh of Egypt. Enemies of old, the two monarchs had brought peace to their lands 13 years before. Now, in order to strengthen the bond between them, Hattusilis was sending his eldest daughter to become the polygamous pharaoh's newest queen. The betrothal had been the subject of more than a year's intensive negotiations, with envoys shuttling back and forth between the Egyptian capital of Pi-Ramses and Hattusilis's distant court.

Daughter—and wife—of Ramses II, Meryetamen is crowned with sacred cobras and sun disks signifying her high status. She wears a collar whose beads are shaped in the hieroglyph for beauty.

To show his wealth, the Hittite ruler had promised not only a princess but also a hefty dowry, including jewels and rich fabrics, bronze ornaments, precious metals, horses, flocks of sheep, herds of cattle, and a troop of talented slaves. For months, Ramses had waited, but neither bride nor bridal gifts had materialized.

Letters, increasingly contentious, traveled between the courts; the pharaoh waxed petulant as time passed and made his displeasure known to his prospective parents-in-law. Hattusilis's feisty consort, Queen Puduhepa, chided Ramses for his impatience, asking—with nearly audible sarcasm—why one of the world's richest monarchs should be so desperate for the promised presents. "My Brother possesses nothing?? That you, my Brother, should wish to enrich yourself from me is neither friendly or honorable!!" She alluded to "various difficulties," including a palace destroyed by fire, as the reasons for the delay.

But by the summer of 1257 BC wedding plans were well under way. Egyptian ambassadors arrived at the Hittite court, at Hattusilis's behest, to perform a ceremony formalizing the betrothal. The queen wrote to Ramses expressing her joy. "When fine oil was poured upon my Daughter's head, the gods of the Netherworld were banished," she said. "On that day, the two great countries became one land, and you the two Great Kings found real brotherhood."

This fascinating exchange of correspondence survived in the Hittite archives—discovered and excavated by the German expedition to Turkey in 1906. The princess's journey to Egypt and the marriage itself were recorded for posterity by Egyptian scribes, who—at Ramses' command—composed a lengthy monograph. Fulsome in its praise of the pharaoh, the text was inscribed on stone monuments erected in Egypt's greatest temples; the Wedding Steles of Ramses II still endure at Karnak, Abu Simbel, and elsewhere, telling the modern world of these long-ago events.

When the bridal party, in all its ponderous magnificence, finally set off for Egypt, Queen Puduhepa accompanied her daughter as far as the border of southern Syria, which was then firmly under Egypt's control. Whatever emotions the two women felt at parting remain unrecorded. But officially the mood was a festive one. The expedition would have been well provisioned or able to rely on the enforced generosity of local potentates who were eager to stay on the pharaoh's good side. The crossing into Egyptian-controlled territory was marked by a great deal of mutual wining and dining among the Hittite and Egyptian delegations.

Though the journey through the mountains and across the plains entailed a winter passage through regions vulnerable to icy blasts, the weather remained unseasonably mild and summery. For this phenomenon—so the Wedding Steles inform—the pharaoh himself deserved full credit. Ramses made a personal appeal to the gods: "The sky is in your hands, the earth is under your feet, whatever happens is what you command—so, may you not send rain, icy blast or snow, until the marvel you have decreed for me shall reach me!"

When the marvel in question reached Pi-Ramses, an event marked by widespread public and private celebrations, her new spouse was enchanted: "Now she was beautiful in the opinion of His Majesty, and he loved her more than anything, as a momentous event for him, a triumph. She was installed in the Royal Palace, accompanying the Sovereign daily, her name radiant in the land." This name, an Egyptian one, Maat-Hor-Neferure, meaning "She who beholds the royal Falcon that is the visible splendor of Re," was new to her.

The honeymoon period so elaborately described in the marriage steles did not, apparently, last a lifetime. During her early years in Egypt, Maat-Hor-Neferure's name and image appeared in conjunction with Ramses' on statues and foundation stones, but after a time she seems to have disappeared from view. The last evidence of her life in Egypt is a fragment of an inventory of clothing and other items from her wardrobe, found by archaeologists at the site of a royal harem that lay 120 miles from Pi-Ramses, on the edge of the garden province of Faiyum.

Beyond these details, little is known of the Hittite bride. But the world she entered is slowly emerging from the shadows. A new generation of Egyptologists has begun to interpret the vast store of surviving texts, images, and artifacts from the ancient civilization along the Nile. In so doing, they have constructed a picture—albeit one sometimes rent by apparent contradictions—of the lives lived by women from every social stratum in the age of Ramses II: great queens commemorated on monumental sculptures, female landowners pursuing their economic interests in well-documented lawsuits, dancers and court musicians painted on the walls of rich men's tombs, prostitutes plying their trade in racy sketches made by daydreaming workmen in the Valley of the Kings.

Taking obvious pleasure in his dynastic obligations, the prolific Ramses fathered more than 90 children during his almost 67-year reign. Their mothers, the women of the royal harems, included at least six chief queens and dozens of lesser wives and concubines. Some—like the Hittite bride and a sister who followed her several years later—were the daughters of foreign kings dispatched to seal a treaty or further a diplomatic alliance; at least one Syrian princess and one Babylonian are mentioned in court correspondence.

Other brides were members in their own right of the Egyptian royal house: Ramses numbered one sister and three daughters among his spouses. Repulsive as it appears to the modern mind, this practice—dating back over a millennium to the time of the Old Kingdom—had deep roots in Egyptian culture and theology. During the New Kingdom, every pharaoh was the son not only of his human father but also of the god Amen, who miraculously manifested his presence in the womb of the queen at the moment of conception. And since Egyptians traced their ancestry matrilineally, marriage to a princess of royal blood would serve to seal the pharaoh's rightful claim to the throne—indeed, some scholars assert that the ruler's divine character in the people's eyes stemmed from such a holy union.

Just as the origins of the pharaoh's wives varied, so, too, did their status at court. Some apparently exercised considerable power and enjoyed high status; others seemed to be little more than conjugal partners. But whatever jockeying for power may have taken place behind the scenes, one woman in the royal household could always be certain of her influence over the pharaoh—Ramses' own mother, Queen Tuya. During the reign of Ramses' father, Seti I, Tuya had apparently lived a life of relative seclusion, not unlike most other queens. Her name does not appear in any texts relating to the great affairs of state, and she is rarely mentioned or pictured on any monuments dating from her husband's lifetime. But as royal widow and queen mother, she entered the limelight. From Pi-Ramses in the Nile Delta to Abu Simbel almost a thousand miles to the south, her son erected statues, and even constructed a temple, in her honor.

On the massive facade of the rock temple at Abu Simbel, she stands in stony grandeur—calf-high against the towering figure of her son—alongside her daughter-in-law Nefertari and assorted royal grandchildren. At Thebes, a small temple that had fallen into disrepair was rebuilt by the pharaoh and dedicated to his mother. Modern scholars speculate that this building once housed a set of carved reliefs found nearby, memorializing Tuya's own parents—the lady Ruia and her husband, Raia, a military man who had risen to the rank of lieutenant of chariotry under a previous pharaoh.

When the long war with the Hittites ended, the queen mother apparently took an active part in the diplomatic ceremonies that confirmed the peace. She, along with Ramses and the high-ranking dignitaries of the court, sent a personal communiqué to the Hittite king, offering her greetings and congratulations. It must have been

The lid from a canopic jar, found in 1972 in the tomb of Ramses II's mother, Tuya, bears an idealized portrait of the queen. Such jars were buried with the royal dead and contained their linen-wrapped organs.

a great moment, witnessing her son's political triumph and knowing that Egypt would—for the first time in decades—be blessed with peace. But her enjoyment was sadly short-lived; she died the next year, a grandmother in her sixties.

Some 3,200 years later, in 1972, a party of French and Egyptian archaeologists found her last resting place, in the Valley of the Queens, west of Thebes. Within the thoroughly looted tomb, they descended a staircase and passed through a series of halls carved out of the rock, until they reached the pillared chamber where her body once lay. The room must have been decorated and furnished with a splendor befitting Tuya's status as wife and mother of pharaohs. Its centerpiece had been the great pink granite sarcophagus that held the mummified queen.

In accordance with Egyptian mummification practice, her vital organs would have been removed from her corpse and preserved in canopic jars. On the lid of one of these vessels, the archaeologists came face-to-face with an idealized image of Tuya herself: a head, some six inches high, carved in alabaster. The face smiled out from beneath a curled wig and a cap, in the form of a vulture, announcing its wearer as a member of the royal house. One of the few other artifacts left behind by the ancient tomb robbers was a bottle of wine deposited in the tomb at the time of the funeral by her loving son.

Not long after the loss of his mother, Ramses had cause to mourn another important woman in his life. At some point in the 24th year of his reign, or soon thereafter, the foremost of his queens, Nefertari, also died. As the monuments that commemorate her life—and the documents that bear her name—attest, she was the first, and seemingly best loved, of Ramses' royal consorts.

Inscriptions record the titles conferred upon her. Some, such as Great Royal Wife and Lady of the Two Lands, namely Upper and Lower Egypt, indicate her official role within the monarchy. Others acknowledge her semidivine status: Nefertari, as chief royal spouse and bearer of Ramses' firstborn son, received the names God's Wife and God's Mother. But the list also includes epithets of a more intimate, affectionate nature, in which the voice of the king himself can be heard, proclaiming her his Lady of Charm, Rich of Praise, Beautiful of Face, and Sweet of Love.

Nefertari's origins are a matter of scholarly debate. She was certainly Egyptian, probably highborn although not necessarily of royal blood. Her parents' names are unknown, although she may have come from a Theban family, as suggested by another of her epithets, Beloved of the Goddess Mut, a deity of Thebes. Her marriage to Ramses is thought to have taken place when he was still heir apparent. She may well have been one of the carefully selected women his father, Pharaoh Seti I, presented to him upon his investiture as prince regent. On an inscription at the temple in Abydos dedicated to his father, Ramses expressed a son's gratitude: "He furnished me with a household of the Royal Harem, comparable with the 'beauties' of the Palace; he chose for me wives."

From the start, Nefertari was first among them. Reliefs on the walls of the shrine at Gebel Silsila, clearly dated to the first year of Ramses' rule, show him and Nefertari officiating jointly in religious ceremonies. The walls of a Nubian temple, built early in the reign, are adorned with images of the couple's eldest son, Amunherwenemef, represented at an age that would suggest he was born before his father ascended the throne. Amunherwenemef was only the first of many offspring: Nefertari bore at least six children, although none, including the young crown prince, survived the venerable Ramses.

During her more than 20-year tenure as chief queen, Nefertari played a conspicuous part in the political and ritual life of the realm. When the landmark treaty between the Egyptian and Hittite thrones was signed, Nefertari exchanged her own official greetings with her opposite number, Queen Puduhepa. The Hittite lady's communiqué, which came first, has not been found, but Nefertari's response still survives: "With me, your sister, all goes well; with my country all goes well. With you, my sister, may all go well; with

This gold death mask covered the face of Kaemwaset, fourth son of Ramses II. A French Egyptologist stumbled upon the crown prince's mummy in 1852 in the Serapeum, a multichambered, underground necropolis reserved for the sacred Apis bulls that cult members believed were the embodiment of the creator god Ptah. Kaemwaset served as a priest of the cult.

In this relief from the temple of Seti I at Abydos, Ramses II prepares to lasso a hobbled bull while Amunherwenemef, his eldest son, tugs on the beast's tail. The animal was intended as a sacrifice, food to nourish the spirit of the pharaoh's father. Of Ramses' numerous royal sons, Merenptah, the 13th, survived long enough to succeed him.

your country may all go well. Behold now, I have noted that you, my sister, have written to me, to enquire after my well-being. May the sun god and storm god bring you joy; and may the sun god cause the peace to be good and give good brotherhood to the great king, the king of Egypt, with his brother the great king, the king of Hatti, forever. And I am in friendship and sisterly relations with my sister the great queen of Hatti, now and forever."

If the monuments known to us portray an accurate picture, it seems clear that no other queen played so conspicuous a part in the life of the realm during Ramses' reign. Nefertari is known to have accompanied Ramses on several royal processions up the Nile, from Pi-Ramses to Thebes, almost 500 miles to the south, to preside jointly with her husband at religious festivals and priestly investitures. At the temples of Karnak, Luxor, and Abu Simbel, sculptors carved her image next to that of her royal spouse.

At Abu Simbel, in Nubia, she was honored above all other queens. Here, Ramses ordered the construction of two massive rock-cut temples, the first dedicated to himself and the official gods of the Egyptian state and the second to Hathor—patroness of motherhood and goddess of love—and his own queen Nefertari. On the facade of this second shrine stands a row of colossal statues: four images of Ramses and two of Nefertari *(pages 106-107)*.

When these great works were completed, probably in 1266 BC, the royal couple and their daughter Meryetamen sailed up the Nile in great magnificence to inaugurate the shrine. On this nearly

1,000-mile journey into the sweltering south, they were accompanied by the viceroy of Nubia, Hekanakht, and a waterborne entourage of courtiers and attendants. To record this glorious event for posterity, the viceroy commissioned a stele to be carved into the rock nearby. Upon its surface, the pharaoh and his daughter are seen performing the appropriate rituals for dedication of the two temples, and Hekanakht appears making his obeisance to a seated Nefertari.

But this great moment in the life of the chief queen may have come near the end of it. Egyptologists speculate that young Meryetamen's newfound prominence may have been due to the fact that her mother, already ailing or fatigued by the journey, was unable to officiate at her husband's side. What is certain is that no later images of Nefertari have come to light, and it is assumed that she died not long after the arduous voyage up the Nile.

Scholars have concluded that, at some point in Ramses' reign, Meryetamen replaced her mother as Great Royal Wife. But neither she nor Nefertari could, in one all-important respect, match the success of their rival Queen Istnofret. Although she appears on few surviving monuments and is rarely mentioned in the extant records of the reign, it was her offspring—Ramses' 13th-born son—who would outlast his long-lived father and inherit the throne as the dynasty's fourth pharaoh, Merenptah.

What little is known about the lives of Ramses' queens comes mostly from the images that appear on monuments, from diplomatic correspondence that has survived in official archives, and from the reliefs and paintings found in temples and royal tombs. They are portrayed fulfilling their official functions, taking part—at the pharaoh's side—in state ceremonies or officiating as high priestesses in religious cults, bearing the ritual objects sacred to particular goddesses within the Egyptian pantheon.

Archaeological evidence about the queens' day-to-day existence is scantier. Excavations by the pioneering English archaeologist Flinders Petrie during the 1880s established the presence of a royal harem at Mi-Wer—to which the Hittite princess who became Queen Maat-Hor-Neferure had eventually retired. Contrary to assumptions, this institution was no mere waiting room for royal consorts, resting between conjugal visits from the king, but a center of agriculture, industry, and education. Full-time, resident administrators

JOURNEYING TOGETHER, FOREVER

For relatives and associates of a pharaoh, life—and death—had certain perquisites. Among the benefits could be the immortality bestowed by a stone funerary monument constructed to outlast the ages. Thus it was that the princess Tia, daughter of Seti I and sister of Ramses II, and her husband, also named Tia, erected a "house of eternity" for themselves at the necropolis of Saqqara near Memphis.

A joint English-Dutch team of archaeologists came across the couple's burial place in 1982 while digging in the area. Looters had long before made off with most of the reusable material, leaving only bits of columns and walls, a side chapel, and the base of a small pyramid *(left)*. Much to the archaeologists' surprise, the tomb turned out to have been shoddily built, despite the prestige and power of its owners. "Hardly a wall is straight," wrote Geoffrey Martin, the leader of the expedition, "and there are scarcely any true right angles." What is more, much of the stone used was of inferior quality, with its faults hidden by plaster.

Still, in its day, the monument, with its pyramid and columned courtyard, must have been impressive. And for all the incompetence of the builders, it did confer the desired immortality. Surviving reliefs adorning the chapel show the couple engaged in various pursuits. On the south wall seen below, for example, they sit serenely together on a bark, pulled by another boat with men in the rigging and horses on deck. They are traveling up the Nile to Abydos to worship, appropriately enough, at the Temple of Osiris.

supervised a staff of specialized artisans and servants. It was the site of textile workshops, devoted to training young women in the crafts of spinning and weaving fine linen cloth and responsible for furnishing garments to the pharaoh's family and its minions. The harem also maintained its own farms and flocks to supply the royal household's grain, milk, and meat.

Important noblewomen of the court also possessed their own personal estates, with a full complement of employees. One surviving document records the rations of herbs, bread, and milk distributed from the estates of Princess Istnofret II to her retainers. Another carries a message to the same princess from two palace singers who seem to have been not merely her servants but also her friends. They ask after her health and well-being, report on their own, and admit that "We're very, very concerned about you!"

At Mi-Wer and other royal residences, including the pharaoh's palace in Pi-Ramses, instructors—possibly veteran bureaucrats and military men retired from active service—taught reading, writing, ethics, etiquette, soldiery, and statecraft. The students included Ramses' own numerous offspring and those of high-ranking Egyptian officials, as well as those children of foreign rulers who had been delivered into the care of the pharaoh to be educated in Egyptian ways. There is some evidence that the daughters of the house may have shared, at least partly, in this schooling.

However industrious, harem life also provided its own abundant comforts and pleasures. Ramses liked to surround himself and his family with beautiful things. His palace interiors at Pi-Ramses and elsewhere gleamed with vibrantly colored tiles and friezes, decorated with fishes and waterfowl *(page 11),* lotuses, and clusters of grapes and poppies.

Whether the king was in attendance or not, there would have been no shortage of delicacies for the royal table. A contemporary training manual for scribes bases a penmanship exercise on what may have been a typical order for a palace banquet celebrating the pharaoh's arrival: "Have made 200 ring-stands for bouquets of flowers, 500 food-baskets. Foodstuff list, to be prepared: 1,000 loaves of fine flour, 10,000 *ibshet*-biscuits, 2,000 *tjet*-loaves; cakes, 100 baskets; dried meat, 100 baskets of 300 cuts; milk, 60 measures; cream, 90 measures; carob-beans, 30 bowls.

A RAMSEAN ARCHITECTURAL WONDER
HIDDEN BENEATH A MODERN TOWN

Meryetamen's statue lies facedown, as it was discovered, in front of the ruined temple-entrance pylon at Akhmim. The large block to the left of her carved figure is a portion of an inscribed pillar belonging to the sculpture of Ramses II.

Workmen protect the hieroglyph-covered base of a statue of a seated Ramses II, believed to have towered some 50 feet. Excavating in Akhmim is complicated by the presence of structures like the one in the background, which has had its wall partially shored up.

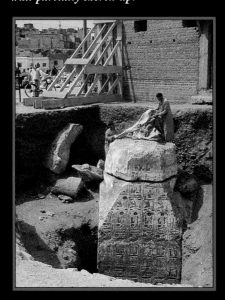

With a past as rich as Egypt's, it can come as no surprise that new finds turn up there year after year; but archaeologists were unprepared for an accidental discovery made in 1981 at Akhmim, a provincial town some 75 miles north of Luxor, site of ancient Thebes. While digging a foundation for a school, laborers uncovered part of a large limestone block, which turned out to be the uppermost portion of a double-plume crown ornament, emblem of either a goddess or a queen. Archaeologists called to the scene dug out the rest of the statue—a 25-foot-long figure of a young woman *(opposite)*. A cartouche revealed the subject's identity as Meryetamen, daughter of Ramses II and his most-favored wife, Nefertari, who later became great royal consort after the queen's death. And an inscription on the base sang Meryetamen's praises, calling her, like her mother, "fair of face, beautiful in the palace, the beloved of the Lord of Two Lands."

Continuing their excavations, the archaeologists unearthed broken pieces of a second massive sculpture, this one of Ramses II. They theorized that works so enormous must have formed part of a vanished temple, perhaps flanking a double-pylon entrance.

Plainly, this was a major find, but the archaeologists were unable to continue their investigations, for to do so would have meant destroying a part of the town. Late in 1991, workers digging yet another foundation happened upon a 50-foot-long, hieroglyph-covered sculpture of Ramses and fragments of a second colossus, apparently that of a woman. More probing revealed ruins of the actual temple to which the sculptures belonged, but once again work came to a halt, and again for the same reason. The inhabitants simply refused to move off the site, even though they were promised new homes by the government. "Antiquities are present in many places," said one. "What have I to do with them? They are nothing but stones." Stones they may be, but the temple beneath Akhmim, the archaeologists now think, may have been even bigger than the temple at Karnak; indeed, its ruins may extend beyond the town's limits. Excavated and restored, the lost temple could become a tourist draw for Akhmim to rival the splendors of Luxor.

Surrounded by scaffolding, the statue of Ramses II's daughter-queen Meryetamen is restored to its upright position. The left hand clutches a menat, a bead necklace with an image of Hathor, goddess of love, music, and dance.

Grapes, 50 sacks; pomegranates, 60 sacks; figs, 300 strings and 20 baskets." To complete the menu, fishermen would deliver the pick of the day's catch from the Nile or the Faiyum Lake, and fowl such as ducks and geese would be plucked and roasted. Leeks, herbs, and honey would be added to please the palate.

At ceremonial dances, or to divert the royal family and guests during such banquets at court, companies of dancers and musicians—usually female—demonstrated their talents. Tomb reliefs, painted pottery, and wall carvings show these entertainers at work. Dancers displayed their acrobatic skills or undulated in a fashion anticipating the techniques of modern Egyptian belly dancers. Musicians provided a rhythmic accompaniment with drums, tambourines, rattles, snapping fingers, and hand-shaped clappers carved of ivory or bone. Orchestral groups and soloists performed on flutes, harps, oboelike reed pipes, and lutes, or they sang. And, as the evening wore on, the cones of perfumed fat worn on the heads of the diners would melt gently into the plaits of their intricately coiffed wigs and the folds of their garments.

Outside the pleasant precincts of the palace, however, life for

In this 18th-Dynasty mural, one of 11 found in the tomb of a Theban official, two girls dance near garlanded wine jugs while two musicians clap their hands and another plays a double flute. On their wigged heads the seated women wear cones of scented ointment that melt and perfume both hair and clothing. The hieroglyphs at top represent lyrics of the song being played.

Ramses' female subjects was very different. Most were peasants, who must have struggled to keep the blowing sands and invasive flies out of their cramped mud houses. They also toiled on the land alongside the men to feed their families on spartan rations of legumes, onions, cheese, and rough bread. In paintings adorning the tombs of their wealthy landlords, women are shown harvesting wheat, picking flax, or hoisting heavy baskets of crops onto their heads for the laborious march from field to storehouse.

Those with a surplus from their own small plots—and a commercial turn of mind—set themselves up as market traders. An illustration in one Theban tomb portrays a female vendor sitting at a well-stocked stall, her wares carefully arranged to catch the buyer's eye. Women were also employed in communal bakehouses, milling flour on an industrial scale. A papyrus listing the production figures for one of these establishments notes that three women—members of a team of 26 millers—gathered 10.5 sacks of grain and ground it into 7.25 sacks of flour in a single day. Other women, like the musicians and dancers who carved out careers at court or traveling between the houses of the rich, boasted specialist skills of their own.

Women dominated the textile industry—second only to agriculture in its importance to the Egyptian economy—and the manufacturing of perfumes derived from pressed lilies and a variety of fragrant botanical oils. Some rose to supervisory positions, possibly in those operations where the work force was mainly or exclusively female: New Kingdom texts identify female overseers of weaving workshops and mention mistress of the wig workshop and mistress of the dining hall. And, as in every society within recorded history, there were women who plied their trade as prostitutes. In the village of Deir el Medina, home base for the workers who built and decorated the tombs in the Valleys of the Kings and Queens on the western bank of the Nile, opposite the religious complex of Thebes, documents refer to those women outside the bonds of nuclear family as "the others." The site has also yielded sketches on limestone or pottery fragments depicting women of easy virtue in various languorous or energetic postures. In the same community, a worker of particularly artistic bent went so far as to produce a papyrus scroll showing, in graphic detail, a busy day in what could only be a brothel.

Other, more conventionally respectable social services, lay almost entirely in the hands of women. Midwifery was a purely feminine concern. At the opposite end of the life cycle, a well-schooled sorority of professional mourners took charge of the obsequies for the dead. Surviving records reveal that these women not only wailed in the approved manner over the departed but also supervised funeral arrangements and negotiated long-term contracts for the performance of memorial rites and the maintenance of tombs.

On their own funerary monuments, many women of Ramses' time identify themselves as priestesses of religious cults dedicated to the worship of particular deities. It is not entirely clear whether those who undertook these activities were professional initiates into the religious community or simply pious laywomen. But, in either case, there were certainly women participating—in great numbers—in religious rites, as the reliefs on temple walls amply demonstrate: In ceremonial scenes, priestess-musicians in the cult of Hathor shake the metal rattles and bead necklaces sacred to the deity of love, who was also the patron of music and dance.

Domestic service undoubtedly provided a major source of livelihood for many women, whether as slaves or free wage earners. In either case, paintings in the tombs of the rich and the royal show female servants carrying dishes for a banquet or dressing a lady's hair.

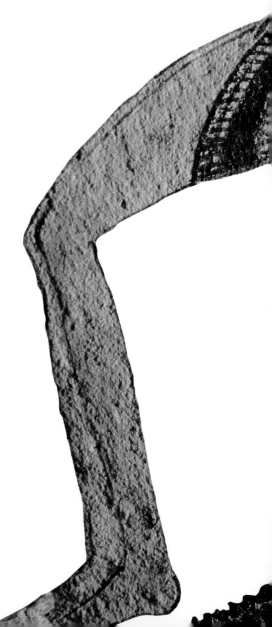

Indeed, so dependent were the upper classes on their household help that they equipped their burial chambers with statuettes of attendants to wait on them in the afterlife. But even families of humbler rank seemed able to afford the services of at least one maid-of-all-work, who might have been paid in food or goods or simply purchased outright as a slave. One such transaction is known through a fragment of papyrus recording a dispute that was brought before the local law court in western Thebes, probably during the 15th or 16th year of Ramses' reign. A woman named Irynofret, wife of a civil servant known as District Officer Simut, purchased a young Syrian slave girl from an itinerant merchant. Probably after some haggling, they agreed on a price, which Irynofret paid in the form of bartered goods: linen dresses, a blanket she had made herself, other household wares, and a collection of copper and bronze vessels.

But shortly after this deal was closed, one of Irynofret's neighbors, a woman named Bakmut, lodged an official complaint: She, not Irynofret, was the owner of some of the goods paid out in exchange for the slave. Therefore, she demanded a share of the girl's services. To back up her claim, she and her husband produced some impressive witnesses: a retired police sergeant from the force entrusted with the protection of the royal tomb, the mayor of western Thebes himself, four of Bakmut's female friends and relations, and even a brother of the defendant's own husband, whose testimony on Bakmut's behalf would certainly not have contributed much to family harmony at Irynofret's house.

Before these witnesses delivered their testimony, the presiding magistrate directed Irynofret to make a formal declaration of her innocence: "Swear an oath by the Sovereign," he ordered, "saying thus: 'If witnesses establish against me that any property of the lady Bakmut was included in [my payment] for this slave-girl, and I have concealed [it], then I shall be liable for 100 strokes, having [also] forfeited her.' "

Irynofret, the record goes on to say, complied with this request and swore her oath, and the witnesses gave their testimony. Unfortunately—and exasperatingly—the rest of the papy-

99

rus has been lost, and the outcome of the case remains unknown.

Some 3,000 years after the lawsuit over the slave girl, in 1886, archaeologists from the Egyptian Antiquities Service came upon a find of remarkable rarity at Deir el Medina: a tomb that had remained intact since the distant day of its sealing, untouched by the thieves who had swooped like carrion crows upon so many houses of the dead on the western bank. Barring access to the burial chamber was a wooden door set in a frame of limestone and secured with a sliding bolt. Upon its surface, scenes painted in deep green, aqua, and red and yellow ocher depicted the tomb's owner, his wife, and children paying homage to various gods and goddesses.

Hieroglyphic inscriptions revealed that the name of the deceased paterfamilias was Sennedjem. His title, Servant in the Place of Truth, identified him as one of the more important people among the workers and artisans at Deir el Medina. When the excavators carefully removed the painted door—the finest of its kind ever to be found on the western bank—and stepped into the burial chamber, they came

Atop one wall of the tomb of an overseer named Sennedjem at Deir el Medina, baboons venerate the sun god Re-Harakhte, as the sun rises from the nether world. Immediately below, Sennedjem and his wife adore Re-Harakhte, Osiris, and Ptah; to the far right a son attends his father's mummy. In the third panel, Sennedjem and his wife reap grain; on the right he is seen sniffing a lotus. In the fourth panel, the couple serenely harvests flax and plows fields.

A vine probably symbolic of birth and rejuvenation adorns the inner coffin of Lady Isis, whose mummy was found in Sennedjem's tomb. Such coffins, presenting the dead in worldly finery, were placed inside a second casket carved to show the deceased as a mummy.

upon not only the late Sennedjem himself but also 19 members of his family, male and female, spanning three generations. Nine bodies rested in wooden coffins, and 11 others lay upon the floor of the tomb, wrapped in layers of white linen.

In one coffin lay a woman named Isis, who may have been a granddaughter or a daughter-in-law married to Sennedjem's son Khabekhnet, whose own burial chamber lay next door. But if this is so, she was not Khabekhnet's only spouse, for his own tomb contained a painted wooden box with an inscription identifying it as the property of Khabekhnet and his wife Sahto.

The images depicted on the walls of Sennedjem's tomb—and the objects found within by the excavators—provide clues about the domestic world inhabited by Isis and the other women in the family: Sahto, her sisters-in-law Tameket and Nefer, and her mother-in-law, Iyneferty. They are dressed in garments of fine, white, pleated linen and wear wigs, probably made of human hair. The cones of perfumed fat atop their heads have melted sufficiently to give their clothes a faintly yellow tinge, which the artist has faithfully reproduced. Following the artistic convention of the period, the painter has given the figures different skin tones according to their sex; Sennedjem and his sons have ruddy complexions, while the women are in paler color.

In the portrait decorating the lid of her inner coffin, Isis displays some of her jewelry. An elaborate collar circles her neck, and two pairs of bone or ivory earrings dangle from her lobes. She wears many rings and bracelets and secures her intricately curled wig with a floral headband.

To pass their leisure hours, the women of the family and their spouses would have occasionally played a popular board game known as senet, in which each opponent moved a set of carved pieces across the squared-off grid of the game board. In New Kingdom burials, this favorite game took on a spiritual significance; in the Sennedjem family tomb, a painting shows Tameket at her husband's side, both intent on a senet game played against an invisible, otherworldly opponent—fate. The prize for which they are apparently contending is the gift of eternal life.

Isis's home, like that of her in-laws, may have been furnished with domestic articles as decorative as they were useful. Jars of multicolored painted pottery—such as a handsome amphora adorned with lotuses, mandrakes, and pomegranates or a pottery vessel decorated with wavy lines to imitate alabaster—held wine, oil, or the

TREASURES FROM THE TEMPLE OF THE LIONESS GODDESS

For centuries, the Egyptian city of Bubastis in the Nile Delta flourished. Named for the lion-headed goddess Bastet, it drew crowds of worshipers to her temples and festivals. Precious metals and semiprecious stones from the East flowed through it and other large cities in the delta in the form of tribute and trade. But by Roman times, Bubastis lay abandoned, the goddess's treasures scattered or destroyed—except for two stashes secreted in the ground. Scholars speculate that priests may have buried them for safekeeping and been unable to reclaim them.

On the morning of September 23, 1906, rumors that railway workers had discovered a hoard of gold and silver vessels the day before swept the town of Zagazig, not far from Tell Basta, the mound containing the ruins of Bubastis. They had stumbled across the treasure while leveling the earth around a temporary rail line at the tell, it was said, and had quietly reburied the find until they could divide the spoils under the cover of night. Galvanized by the story, the Egyptian Antiquities Service and local police searched the homes of those suspected of involvement.

From a dealer who had not had time to pass his acquisitions on, they confiscated a beautiful silver jug with a gold handle cast in the shape of a goat *(opposite)* and portions of a silver vase. From inside the ceiling of a worker's home, they retrieved a gold cup bearing the cartouche of Queen Tausert, the final ruler of the 19th Dynasty. But the rest of the treasure sadly eluded the authorities.

Believing similar finds might get into the wrong hands, C. C. Edgar of the Egyptian Antiquities Service began a controlled excavation of the tell. At first diggers uncovered only a scattering of small objects. One of these, a gold-leafed piece of silver, had to be excavated a second time from a worker's mouth, where it had been concealed. Then on October 17, a supervisor spotted a laborer laying bare some silver fragments and called in help to protect the promising site.

Further digging exposed a second cache, consisting of finely crafted ritual vessels, exquisite jewelry, and rings, pins, and wine strainers. But there was nothing to equal the recovery of a pair of gold bracelets that had belonged to Ramses II, among the few personal items of his to have reached modern times intact. Thanks to the bracelets and Tausert's cartouche on the gold cup, the Tell Basta finds could be dated to the Ramesside era.

Almost perfectly preserved, these magnificent gold bracelets, adorned with ducks that are fashioned from gold and lapis lazuli, give Ramses' name. Both women and men frequently wore several sets of such ornamental bands.

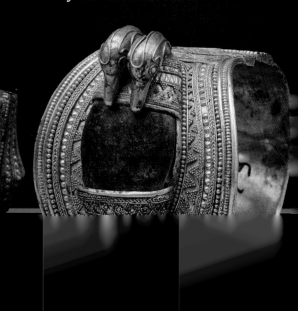

Multiple-row necklaces were the ancient Egyptians' most ubiquitous item of jewelry, as evidenced by their statues and tomb paintings. This gold and carnelian necklace, discovered in tiny pieces, was restrung based on a similar necklace carved on a statue of one of Ramses' daughters.

A gold goat perches on his hind legs to sip at the edge of a silver vase, a ring for hanging the vessel attached to his nose. This delightful vase displays Egypt's cosmopolitan nature in its pomegranate shape—a Levantine fruit foreign to Egypt—and its silver and gold, metals usually imported from the Near East and Nubia to the south.

As depicted in this painted wood figure from the 19th Dynasty, the god Bes shakes a tambourine while dancing on a lotus flower, symbol of regeneration. He was believed to ward off demons during childbirth and to bring happiness to the home, where his likeness was incorporated into headrests, mirrors, and other items.

scented fat for perfume cones. Lidded chests were cunningly painted to give the illusion of ivory and the grain of rare woods.

The information provided by the family tomb about the world of Sennedjem's female relatives is only a starting point. Other contemporary burials and a wealth of written documentation supplement the picture. It is possible, for instance, to make a fairly accurate guess about the items that Isis would have stored in one of those artfully painted wooden boxes: linens, jewelry, and cosmetics.

Women and men alike used makeup, outlining their eyes with kohl for the sake of appearance and for protection from the fierce Egyptian sun. They kept their skins soft with oils and unguents made from various animal and vegetable ingredients and rouged their cheeks with a mixture of fat and red ocher.

Smelling fresh and sweet was a matter of some concern. The reasonably affluent washed daily, starting the day with a shower of cool water, poured from a servant's pitcher and enriched with such cleansing ingredients as natron—a naturally occurring sodium carbonate (used also for mummification). Poorer folk, without the means to purchase either natron or the servant to apply the dissolved salt, employed a mix of ash and animal fat as an inexpensive version of soap. To prolong the effect of these ablutions, a woman of Isis's means would have applied a deodorant made from turpentine, incense, and a scented powder of unknown composition. As a finishing touch, she might have doused herself with her choice of perfumes: Her taste might run to a straightforward essence of pressed lotus blossoms or—if Khabekhnet's income from private jobs in addition to his tomb-building work allowed—a costlier and more exotic blend of myrrh, frankincense, broom, and an assortment of extracts from plants grown in foreign lands.

A medical papyrus supplies a recipe that Isis might have followed if she wanted to keep her breath sweet. "Dry oliban, pine seeds, terebinth resin, fragrant reed, cinnamon rind, melon, Phoenician reed. Grind finely, mix into a solid mass and put on the fire. Add honey to it. Heat, knead, make into pellets." From the same or similar texts, she could have also derived formulas for getting rid of pimples and other minor blemishes. To reduce wrinkles, she would rub her face with a paste of finely ground terebinth-tree rubber, wax, a special grass imported from the Mediterranean island of Cyprus, and freshly pressed oil. Other compounds served less salubrious objectives; one text gives helpful instructions for a potion of burnt lotus leaves steeped in oil that could be placed on a female enemy's head to make her hair fall out.

If she were worried about her health, Isis would have consulted a physician. Texts written for professional practitioners covered most areas of general medicine, with chapters concentrating on complaints that ranged from depression to what may have been venereal diseases, and perhaps even cancer. One manual gives a therapy for a woman afflicted with a profound lethargy, "who wants to lie down, making no effort to get up, and being unwilling to shake it off. You should say about her: This is spasms of the womb. You should treat her as follows: Make her drink a pint of *haawy*-fluid and make her vomit it at once."

Many women consulted doctors for fertility problems, and the medical literature gave instructions for assessing her chances of conception. "To ascertain whether or not a woman will have a child: the herb *bededu-ka,* powdered and soaked in the milk of a woman who has borne a son. Let the patient eat it, if she vomits it, she will bear a child, if she has flatulence, she will not bear."

If and when Isis did conceive, she would turn to a midwife rather than a physician to help her through the labor. For a normal childbirth, the midwife arrived at the house of the mother with a specially designed wooden birthing chair, equipped with a semicircular seat and two upright rods that the mother could grasp for support while bearing down to push the baby out. In cases of prolonged labor, the midwife might resort to stimulants, either applied externally to the lower abdomen or prepared as a cordial for the expectant mother to drink. According to one medical papyrus, the ingredients that might be used in such situations included salt, honey, oil, wine, incense, and various herbs or vegetables, sometimes combined with the pulverized shells of tortoises or scarab beetles.

Even with such expert assistance, birth had its dangers for mother and child alike. Modern researchers have estimated that in ancient Egypt some 25 mothers out of every 1,000 died in the course of, or soon after, giving birth—comparable to the figures for rural England between the 16th and 18th centuries AD.

Facing such dangers, Isis and her contemporaries might be inclined to improve their chances of survival by praying to one of the deities associated with childbirth: the goddess Hathor, venerated as a special patron and guardian of the female sex; the hippopotamus goddess Taweret; or Bes, a deity associated with affairs of the home and hearth, whose ugliness was regarded as a useful deterrent to malevolent demons. Various forms of magic could also assist: One papyrus suggests that to alleviate intense labor pains, the woman's attendants should utter certain incantations over a clay figurine and place it on the mother's forehead.

The archaeological record fails to reveal whether Isis was happy in her marriage, but had she not been, divorce was an option available to Egyptian women of the day. They enjoyed the same rights as their husbands to terminate a marriage that had gone awry. The division of joint property and the allocation of any dowry the woman had brought with her to the union would depend on whether the male or female partner had initiated the proceedings.

In other respects, women also enjoyed full equality under the law. Numerous surviving legal documents attest that they had the right to own property—indeed, land was handed down through the female line—and to dispose of it through lease, sale, or other legal agreements without the need of any male agent or guardian to act on their behalf. One papyrus even registers a land sale by a consortium of female owners, acting together. Similarly, the case between Irynofret and her neighbor over the slave girl makes it clear that the property—and the legal dispute—rested with the two females; their husbands were only witnesses, with no liability of their own. A woman could also adopt children in her own right, witness legal documents, and act as executrix for wills. In ancient Egypt, obtaining justice in the courts depended more on social class and family wealth than sex.

Yet, even for female members of the richest and most powerful families, abstract legal rights did not guarantee equal status. The attitudes toward women reflected in Egyptian literature reveal considerable ambivalence—and sometimes outright misogyny. In mythology, the great goddesses embody danger as well as virtue; Hathor protects but also imperils by her terrible anger, and Isis is simultaneously a nurturing mother goddess and a sorceress with frightening powers. In fictional narratives of a more secular sort, female characters commonly appear as treacherous figures who seduce, betray, and murder to satisfy their wicked lusts.

In the popular literary genre known as wisdom texts, Egyptian authors passed codes of manners and mores from one generation

Feathers and the solar disk and horns of the goddess Hathor crown one of two colossi of Nefertari that, flanked by figures of Ramses, guard the entrance (center) *to the small temple at Abu Simbel. An inscription on the buttresses of the monument boasts that nothing commensurate to these figures had been made before.*

to the next, using the conventional form of a father's instructions to his son. In these texts—some dating back to the Old Kingdom, nearly 1,000 years before Ramses' reign—women were also treated warily, especially when they were not firmly under a man's control. "Do not go after a woman," one author enjoined. "Let her not steal your heart. Beware of a woman who is a stranger. Don't stare at her when she goes by; do not know her carnally." A creature like this, the writer pronounced, is "a deep water whose course is unknown. Such is a woman away from her husband. When she has no witness, she is ready to ensnare you."

Safely ensconced in marriage and motherhood, the female sex became worthier of respect. "Do not control your wife in her house," commanded one writer, "when you know that she is efficient." And, whatever the distractions of married bliss, a man's mother should not be forgotten: "Support her as she supported you; she had a heavy load in you. But she did not abandon you." A woman's social position was defined by that of her husband. On at least one point of etiquette, a New Kingdom wisdom text summarized a practice that is still much in evidence more than 3,000 years later: "A woman is asked about her husband; a man is asked about his rank."

In family tombs and on funerary monuments, the same ethos applied. The male head of the family is always identified as the tomb's owner and memorialized with an inscription recording his personal history, the offices he

held, and the high points of his career. Wives and daughters receive shorter shrift. Apart from being identified by their relationship to the tomb owner, they are given, at best, only the briefest descriptions, such as "mistress of the house" or "chantress" of a particular deity's cult. When married couples are shown, either seated or engaged in an act of worship, the man is nearly always portrayed on the right-hand side of the image, which—according to the canons of ancient Egyptian art—represented the predominant position.

Observing these distinctions, some present-day Egyptologists warn against the assumption that ancient Egypt was some form of proto-feminist paradise. They point out that all the information and images that have come down to us—from documents to the art on tomb and temple walls—have probably been the work of male creators and interpreters: the sculptors at work on royal monuments or the bureaucratic scribes of court or temple.

Only rarely in the surviving words and pictures from Ramses' age are heard the voices of women themselves. There is a papyrus letter from a Theban woman named Hennutawy to her husband, a scribe. In his absence, she had assumed his duties of dispensing grain to the town's inhabitants—and had uncovered discrepancies in the units of measure used by the workers. "I went my own self and caused the grain to be received while I was there. It amounted to 146.75 *khar*-measures by this *oipe*-measure."

The men protest their innocence, assuring her the total had come to 150 khar-measures when weighed out on the oipe-measure at the granary. "I checked out the *oipe*-measure and told them, 'I'm satisfied with the check. I shall find the grain wherever it is,' so I said to them." And the tone of her letter sounds as though she means it.

In a personal aside to her husband in this mostly businesslike letter, Hennutawy writes, "Now don't worry about your father. I've heard that his condition is very good." Still reassuring him, she adds, "The steward of Amen has written me saying, 'Don't worry about him. He is all right; he is in health. No harm has befallen him.' "

Unfortunately, writings by women such as Hennutawy are scarce. Yet, despite their apparent silence, Egyptian women could still affect the course of history. One of Ramses' most celebrated namesakes and successors would discover this to his cost, when a conspiracy hatched in the harem, among his malcontented minor wives, would sow the seeds of his destruction and hasten his dynasty's end.

A LIVING TOMB

The air is amazingly still and cool, even in midsummer, stars twinkle on the dark blue ceiling, and the brightly colored figures on the walls stand frozen midscene like players in a perpetual drama on a stage where time has stopped. This so-called house of eternity in the Valley of the Queens was the burial place of Ramses II's favorite wife, Nefertari, "The Most Beautiful of Them."

Following tradition, the tomb's wall paintings represented far more than mere decoration: They were intended as magical depictions of the rituals necessary for achieving everlasting life in the nether world. To ensure, then, a speedy and certain transition to immortality for the revered queen, artists of ancient Thebes created 5,600 square feet of images—among the most exquisite in Egypt. Indeed, the paintings, with their vivid depictions of Nefertari on her quest for eternity, her face subtly carved into the plaster and shaded for depth *(above)*, ex-

hibit a degree of realism rarely seen in Egyptian art.

The Italian archaeologist Ernesto Schiaparelli discovered the looted tomb in 1904, empty except for a few small artifacts and in a state of disrepair. Carved from poor-quality limestone 40 feet below ground, the walls had to be plastered to ensure a smooth and even surface for the artists. Over the centuries, the plaster began to separate from the rock, and the paint peeled, flaked, and chipped. Although some repairs were made after the tomb's discovery, the deterioration accelerated until the 1980s, when a study estimated that one-fifth of the murals were irreparably damaged. In 1986 the Egyptian Antiquities Organization (EAO) teamed up with the Getty Conservation Institute (GCI) of Los Angeles in a multinational effort to preserve, but not reconstruct, this remarkable piece of Egypt's patrimony. The fascinating story of that effort is told on the following pages.

THROUGH THE EYES OF THE BEHOLDERS

Opening the tomb of Nefertari in 1904, Ernesto Schiaparelli instantly recognized the phenomenal artistic importance of his find. And, as one of a new breed of archaeologists mindful of the scientific and curatorial aspects of his work, Schiaparelli supervised the creation of a permanent record of the site. Don Michele Pizzio, an ordained priest who was the team's photographer, produced, in conjunction with the famed Egyptologist Francesco Ballerini, 132 glass-plate negatives of both the interior and exterior of the tomb. This historic collection of photographs remains the richest source of information about the wall paintings at the time of their discovery.

Additional photographic images, taken over the years, documented the continuing deterioration of the murals and attempts at restoration. The photos ranged from the archival, such as Harry Burton's series for the Metropolitan Museum of Art's Egyptian expedition in the 1920s *(below)*, to the more mundane, in the form of tourist postcards. The resulting pictorial record proved invaluable to the conservators beginning work on the tomb in 1986. Examined chronologically, the images revealed erroneous alterations made by previous restorers and aided in the accurate replacement of pieces of plaster that had dropped from the walls and ceiling. To fully document the recent work, as well as to provide a benchmark for the future, the Mexican photographer Guillermo Aldana shot some 7,000 pictures of the tomb before, during, and after the conservation effort.

Nefertari holds a symbol of royal power over a mound of slaughtered oxen, food for the creator god Atum. The offerings are seen virtually in their entirety in the 1920s photograph taken by Harry Burton for the Metropolitan Museum (left). By the time the EAO/GCI team began their work, a large portion of the tomb's paintings had deteriorated, and what remained was obscured by a coat of dust, as evidenced by the scene above. The team's meticulous cleaning and consolidation techniques resulted in the vastly improved condition of the scene in 1992 (above, right).

Photographer Guillermo Aldana captures on film the murals lining the tomb's stairway. Over the entrance to the burial chamber, Maat, goddess of truth and order, spreads her brilliant blue-green wings—a gesture of protection for the dead queen.

ASSESSING THE DAMAGE

"hen a conservator sees something in bad condition, he has to put it in good condition. It is a desire to set things right." With these words, world-renowned conservator Professor Paolo Mora summed up his first impression of Nefertari's tomb and his commitment to its preservation. The EAO/GCI conservation team, codirected by Mora and his wife, Laura, worked in tandem with a multidisciplinary group of scientists to arrest the runaway damage to the paintings.

The team members began the conservation project by conducting a comprehensive scientific analysis of the site. Specialists in various fields investigated the geology and hydrology of the surrounding valley, analyzed the effects on the tomb of variations in humidity and temperature, checked for microscopic algal and bacterial contamination, and determined the composition of all original materials using x-rays and chemical and spectrographic tests. At the same time, the Moras and their crew produced line drawings of each wall painting, pinpointing and color-coding the location, nature, and degree of damage.

With this preliminary information in hand, the con-

servation team undertook emergency measures to prevent further loss until an overall plan could be devised. They attached strips of delicate Japanese mulberry-bark paper to weakened or damaged sections of the walls and ceiling to combat the most serious problems: falling plaster and flaking paint. The securing of heavier ceiling fragments sometimes required the application of a fine-gauge cotton gauze. In all, the conservators affixed more than 10,000 of the protective paper and cloth bandages, some of which can be seen adhering to the image of the goddess below.

The workers then proceeded to clean the painted surfaces, which were covered not only with dust but also with grime and cobwebs. Since the fragility of the walls precluded use of any tools that might cause damage of their own, a low-pressure air gun was employed to blow away the buildup. Surprisingly, during the initial cleaning of the tomb a tiny piece of a woman's gold bracelet inscribed with hieroglyphs was discovered. Study revealed that the piece was coated with a mummification resin, suggesting that the bracelet may have been worn by Nefertari to the grave.

Early restorers covered badly damaged murals with facings of heavy cotton gauze held in place with a strong adhesive (above). The subsequent removal of the gauze involved painstaking, arduous labor, with repeated applications of solvent to dissolve the glue (left).

Conservators inject acrylic-resin emulsion behind loose ceiling fragments to prevent their detachment (right). The team members used only soluble fixatives to ensure reversibility, if warranted in the future.

COMBATING THE DESTRUCTIVE FORCES

The myriad tests conducted by the multidisciplinary specialists of the EAO/GCI conservation project revealed many factors that had contributed to the deterioration of the wall paintings. Water seepage, earthquakes, vandalism, and even bacterial growth all caused damage to the tomb. The main culprit, however, was found to be none other than sodium chloride—common salt.

The limestone rock out of which Nefertari's tomb was hewn contains salts that when moistened leach out and crystallize between the rock, the plaster, and the paint, forcing the layers apart. Water first entered the tomb in the wet plaster applied to the walls. Archaeological probing of the area around the tomb uncovered evidence of torrential downpours, especially during Roman times. The more recent hazard, however, was the moisture emitted by visitors as they breathed and perspired in the close space of the tomb, which spurred the formation of salt crystals.

To prevent the total and permanent loss of the paintings, the conservation team took painstaking measures *(below)*. Working in the cooler months of five successive years, they used scalpels, hammers and chisels, and microdrills to remove intrusive materials—mainly salt crystals but also dirt, decayed plaster, and cement introduced in earlier interventions—from beneath the cracking painted surface. They reattached fallen and dangling plaster with salt-free mortar mixed from local sand and gypsum, using ancient Egyptian methods. The conservators also rebonded flaking paint to plaster with water-soluble acrylic resin or a mild solvent. The conservation program ended with a final cleaning and removal of any remaining foreign substances, including some paint used in previous restoration efforts. Throughout the course of the project, the team remained faithful to their goal of minimal intervention in order to retain the historical integrity of Nefetari's tomb.

As salt crystals grow, they push surfaces away from the rock, as here. Conservators dubbed the crystallization on one piece "Manhattan" because of its skyline profile.

Gingerly holding a layer of decoratively painted plaster hanging from the wall, a conservator loosens salt crystals and old cement with a chisel.

Low-pressure air guns, such as this one, facilitate the removal of dirt and debris from behind partially detached pieces of plaster so that they might be fixed to the wall.

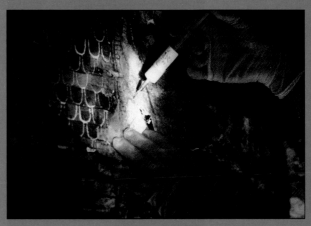

After new mortar is applied to the rock wall, it is injected with a solution designed to slow down the setting time and prevent the absorption of moisture by the plaster.

A tension-held press holds a polyurethane strut against the reattached fragment, keeping it in place until the mortar has completely dried, about 48 hours.

A detail depicting Osiris's foot displays final results of the procedures tracked in the preceding four photos. No attempt was made to fill the blank areas with repainting.

A NEW LEASE ON ETERNITY

A visitor to Nefertari's tomb today would be struck by the amazing freshness of its paintings and the brightness of their hues. Once again, crisp outlines reveal the queen's shapely form, seen through her diaphanous gowns. So, too, inscriptions from Egyptian funerary literature read with their original clarity. Painterly brush strokes are evident, as well as a few inadvertent reminders of the ancient artists. Here and there brush hairs lodge in pigment, and splatters abound. Even fingerprints left in the then-wet paint can be seen.

But having saved the murals, the conservators faced a problem. Environmental monitoring showed that 12 people in the tomb for one hour increased humidity by 5 percent and that levels as low as 50 percent could reactivate the salt crystallization process. As a result of this study, authorities hope that in the future the number of visitors allowed inside the tomb will be strictly controlled. Meanwhile, the leopard-skin-clad Horus and striped *djed*-pillars on the columns still surround the spot where Nefertari's pink granite sarcophagus rested. And once more, through the diligence of mortals, her tomb expresses the idea of eternity. Long live the queen!

F O U R

EGYPT'S DESCENT INTO CHAOS

Known in the shorthand of archaeologists as KV7—for Kings' Valley 7—it is just one of scores of similarly numbered tombs that honeycomb the cliffs on either side of the long, narrow defile the ancient Egyptians knew as the Great Place. Here, in a parched and desolate valley, the dead pharaohs of the New Kingdom were consigned to eternity, each ritually sheltered in an elaborate vault and surrounded by the trappings that would ease the passage into the afterlife.

But like most of its neighboring tombs, KV7 is today quite literally the dustbin of history, its corridors and chambers choked with tons of silt and debris deposited over the past three millennia by rare flash floods brought on by torrential downpours. Indeed, in places the huge 8,800-square-foot tomb is filled with sediment to within a few feet of the ceiling.

The devastation is evident throughout the ancient tomb. In the vault's Hall of Waiting, for example, a well shaft sunk into the floor is also plugged with flood debris. Beyond, a long passageway slopes downward toward yet another room, known as the Hall of Truth, which in turn leads to the heart of the tomb, the burial chamber itself. Inside this chamber stands a thicket of shattered pillars that once supported an arched, 23-foot-high ceiling. Wide cracks have opened in the walls, the result of successive cycles of

Ramses III—the last great warrior king of the New Kingdom—clutches his enemies by the hair in reliefs flanking the doorway and windows of this tower gate, the main entrance to the pharaoh's fortified mortuary temple at Medinet Habu.

119

flooding and drying. A few steps away, in one of several side chambers, fragments of plaster have fallen from the decorated ceiling and now litter the surface of the flood sediment.

Kings' Valley 7's present condition offers scarcely a hint of the tomb's former splendor or of its illustrious owner. For it was through these corridors, in the autumn of 1224 BC, that the mummified corpse of Ramses II, resplendent in its nested coffins, was borne by torchlight to be installed in a stone sarcophagus in the pillared burial chamber. Once their task was done, the priests and officials of the funeral procession left as they had entered, brushing away their footsteps, dousing the torches, then barricading the entrance with masonry and sealing it for an imagined eternity.

Ramses' death around the age of 90 brought to an end a reign that had lasted almost 67 years and had marked yet another golden age in a land with an already long and lustrous history. Yet even as the body of the dead king was laid to rest, the empire he had done so much to forge was itself edging into the shadows of history. For Egypt, the path ahead—like the entrance to Ramses II's tomb—led forward but inexorably downward. And, like the pharaoh's tomb, what had once been splendid would in the end lie in ruins.

Richard Fazzini, field director in 1975 of a joint investigation by the Brooklyn Museum and the American Research Center in Egypt of KV7, the ruined tomb of Ramses II, examines decoration surviving in one of the flood-damaged rooms. Assessment of the feasibility of future work in KV7 led to the museum's 1978-1979 Theban Royal Tomb Project that studied the effect humans, local geological factors, and sporadic heavy rains have had on tombs in the Valley of the Kings.

Still, the end of empire would have been far from the thoughts of Ramses' 13th and eldest surviving son, the stocky Merenptah, who was in his sixties when he ascended the Egyptian throne. Before long, however, the new pharaoh faced the first of a number of challenges to his authority, as revolts in neighboring Canaan and southern Syria threatened Egypt's borders for the first time in nearly half a century. To his credit, Merenptah acted quickly to crush the rebellion, then celebrated his triumph in a series of battle reliefs carved on the walls of the temple at Karnak.

The walls of Karnak also record a far more serious threat to Egypt's sovereignty. In the fifth year of Merenptah's reign, a massive incursion of Libyans and so-called Sea Peoples breached the empire's western defenses. No ordinary raiding party, the invaders had evidently entered Egypt with every intention of staying, undaunted by having picked a fight with one of the superpowers of the day. The Libyan leader, a man named Meryre, for example, brought along all of his possessions and his entire family. For their part, the Sea Peoples—not a lone culture but the advance wave of a great human

migration that would engulf the civilizations of the Mediterranean in the decades ahead—also shared in the invasion.

Although the surviving records are vague about the exact location of the ensuing battle, the invaders met the pharaoh's army somewhere in the western part of the Nile Delta early on a spring morning in 1220 BC. For six hours, while Merenptah held his foot soldiers and charioteers in reserve, Egyptian archers rained arrows on the enemy, slaughtering the Libyans and their allies where they stood. Those who lived to retreat were then hunted down by the Egyptian chariotry and infantry. Even so, Libyan leader Meryre managed to escape, casting off his footwear in his haste to get away, if one account is taken literally. "The wretched chief of Libya," reads the inscription, "his heart was paralyzed with fear, it shrank, he stopped and knelt down leaving his bow and quiver and sandals on the ground behind him." The victorious Egyptians proceeded to count the number of enemy dead—some 6,000 in all—in the usual manner, lopping a hand from the corpses of the circumcised and severing the phallus of those who did not follow this Egyptian custom *(page 129)*.

But while Merenptah's troops had been marching northwest to fight the Libyans, word came of trouble in the south, where, after seven decades of peace, Egypt's subjects in lower Nubia had revolted. Suppression was swift and ruthless. Afterward, as the inscription on a stele from Merenptah's time makes clear, ordinary Egyptians could again "walk the roads at any pace without fear," farmers could return to the fields, and towns that had been emptied in panic could once again be settled. "Re has returned to Egypt," concludes the inscription, its chiseled symbols expressing the collective gratitude of a nation to its god.

The remainder of Merenptah's short reign of a decade was

At far right in this illustration from the Great Harris Papyrus, Ramses III greets the main deities of Memphis—(from right to left) Ptah, god of creativity; Sekhmet, Ptah's wife and protector; and Nefertem, their son. The holy staffs held by the deities may be gnomons, gauges for determining through the shadows they cast the height of the sun, the time of day, and even the season.

apparently peaceful. But for Egyptologists, the period immediately following this pharaoh's death presents a puzzle, since, based on the evidence that is available, it appears that the rightful line of succession was broken by an interloper by the name of Amenmesse. Unfortunately, that evidence, which is frequently at odds with itself, precludes a definitive verdict about whether Merenptah was followed directly by Amenmesse. Most scholars, however, accept this theory and see Amenmesse's ascent as proof of a power struggle between two rival factions seeking the throne: the offspring of Merenptah and the many still-living children of the prolific Ramses II. Amenmesse may have numbered among the latter.

Exactly how Amenmesse might have seized ruling power remains a mystery, but this pharaoh's brief reign precipitated almost two decades of dynastic intrigue and civil strife. Indeed, after less than four years, Amenmesse was apparently succeeded by the very man he had previously usurped, the crown prince Seti-Merenptah, who assumed the throne as Seti II. The new pharaoh wasted little time in rewriting history by systematically obliterating the name of Amenmesse from monuments all over Egypt.

But Seti himself ruled for merely six years. An inscription on a limestone chip, or ostracon, now in the Egyptian Museum in Cairo indicates that Seti II was succeeded by a teenaged son, Siptah. The boy's youth and frail health, however, gave the widowed queen Tausert just the excuse that she needed to wield power in his stead.

The unfortunate Siptah died within six years, at the tender age of about 20, and in the absence of any legitimate heir, Tausert was now able to rule in her own right—becoming only the fourth female pharaoh in the last thousand years. Yet Tausert's days, too, were numbered; within two years both her reign and the 19th Dynasty itself—the direct line of Ramses II—came to an end.

The best evidence that the years following the death of Ramses II were a time of great turmoil for Egypt comes from a document called the Great Harris Papyrus, preserved today in the British Museum. The 133-foot-long scroll was composed in 1165 BC by Ramses IV to commemorate the death of his father, Ramses III. "The land of Egypt was cast adrift, every man being a law unto himself and they had no leader for many years," the papyrus says of the dark days at the end of the 19th Dynasty, perhaps with a little exaggeration. "Each joined with his neighbor in plundering their goods, and they treated the gods as they did men."

With disorder persistent, fighting sometimes spread throughout Thebes, as Egyptian clashed with Egyptian. Even within the tightly knit community of Deir el Medina, the tomb makers feuded violently among themselves, splitting into factions that seemed to mirror, on a much smaller scale, the rivalries within their government. Moreover, while most of the tomb makers struggled to keep up with the demand for enough tombs to accommodate the rapid turnover of monarchs, others were accused of violating the sanctity of the Valley of the Kings by pocketing tools or pinching building materials, and sometimes even the unthinkable—plundering the treasures in the tombs themselves.

For all its problems, however, Egypt could at least take comfort in the continued security of its borders. Elsewhere throughout the Mediterranean, one country after another was being overrun by a tide of barbarians as the 13th century BC drew to a close. "No land could stand before their arms," lamented inscriptions on the walls of the temple complex at Medinet Habu. By 1200 BC even Egypt's former enemy and more recent ally the Hittite Empire—for decades a bulwark against barbarian expansion from the north and west—was itself about to go under. A short time later, the written records that had until now so thoroughly documented the rise of Hittite power suddenly ceased. Modern-day excavations confirm that around this

A brilliantly colored pictorial representation of Egyptian cosmology, shown here in a watercolor reconstruction, adorned the right entrance to the palace at Medinet Habu. The red sun god spreads protective wings over portrayals of Ramses III as a blue sphinx crushing his enemies. Faience tiles of vanquished foreigners (enlarged, right) stylishly fill the bottom row.

MEDINET HABU'S ENDURING MYSTERY: WHO WERE THE PEOPLES OF THE SEA?

By all accounts, the end of the 13th century BC was a tumultuous time around the Mediterranean. Battles and conflagrations raged in Anatolia, the Levant, Cyprus, and mainland Greece. Aggressors headed toward Egypt in ships, while others, journeying by foot, had set their sights on the green and fertile lands of the Nile. But Ramses III, already facing attacks from the Libyans, drove the interlopers back.

Who were these people? Egyptian artists depicted the traditional enemies of the country—Libyans, Hittites, Nubians, and Syrians—on the walls of Ramses's mortuary temple at Medinet Habu, but inscriptions there identified others as the Sea Peoples. Some were named specifically, among them the Peleset, Tjekker, Shekelesh, and Denyen. As homeless wanderers seeking a place to settle, they have gone down in history with their names intact but their origins unclear.

Modern scholars trying to identify the marauders turned to etymology and Mediterranean archaeology for clues. Linguistic similarities between names led researchers to propose ties between Peleset and Philistine, Weshesh and Troy's Wilusa, and Shekelesh and Sicilian. More concretely, round shields and horned helmets found in Sardinia matched those used by Sherden warriors in Medinet Habu depictions. But physical corroborations are few, for the temple's decorations were not meant to be a historical record as much as a paean to a pharaoh who hoped to be known forever as the king who saved Egypt from the Sea Peoples.

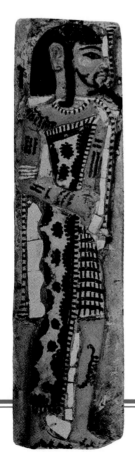

LIBYAN   **NUBIAN**   **SYRIAN**   **PALESTINIAN BEDOUIN**   **HITTITE**

same time Hatti, the Hittite homeland, was utterly destroyed, its cities burned to the ground.

The barbarians responsible for the sudden collapse of much of Mediterranean civilization included some of the same Sea Peoples who, a generation earlier, had penetrated Egypt's borders with their Libyan allies only to be soundly defeated by Merenptah. Now, even as Sethnakht, the first pharaoh in Egypt's 20th Dynasty, prepared to take the throne, these "northerners coming from all lands," as Egyptian sources described them, turned envious eyes on the fertile Nile valley in their search for new territory.

As fate would have it, the Sea Peoples were not to be Sethnakht's problem. A shadowy figure of obscure origins, who, in the words of the Great Harris Papyrus, had been chosen by the gods "to put the land in its proper state," Sethnakht reigned for perhaps two years, living only long enough to make a start on his divine mission. Then, sometime around 1196 BC, he left the crown in the more capable hands of his son Ramses III.

Although little is known of the early days of Ramses III's reign, by year five the new pharaoh was fighting the first of a number of wars—not, as might be expected, against the Sea Peoples, but against an old enemy, the Libyans, and their neighbors the Meshwesh. That war, like those that would follow it, is chronicled in detail on the walls of the Ramses III's mortuary temple at Medinet Habu, on the west bank of the Nile opposite Thebes *(page 129)*.

Even in their present ruined state these walls describe a time when the Libyans, covetous as always of the rich lands of the Nile, in spite of their defeat at the hands of Merenptah, were again encroaching on the western edges of the delta. After consulting the oracle of Amen at Thebes, Ramses ordered his armies to meet the invaders. Thousands of Libyans died in the ensuing battle. The Egyptians tallied the enemy dead in the usual manner, with severed body parts, which were heaped up in front of Ramses' royal chariot. More than a thousand prisoners were also taken, branded as slaves, and paraded through the Egyptian capital.

Ramses had little time to savor his victory, however, before facing his next challenge, this time from the troublesome Sea Peoples. Once again the walls at Medinet Habu tell the story, recounting how the enemy moved against Egypt by land and sea from the direction of Syria. But those who approached by sea fared no better than the Libyans and the Meshwesh had.

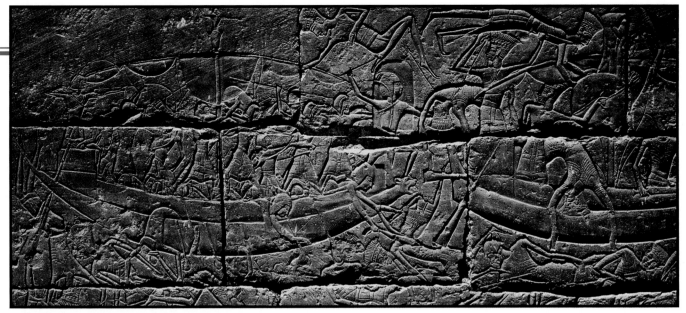

Egyptians on a boat adorned with the lioness head of Sekhmet, goddess of war, holding an enemy in her mouth, use slings and bows to repel the Sea Peoples in the scene above, part of a massive relief at Medinet Habu. The rest of the carving, rendered below, details how the Egyptians capsized one of the enemy boats (center) and took many of the invaders prisoner (bottom).

Reliefs at the temple at Medinet Habu depict the Sea Peoples attacking in ships powered only by sails, with prows carved into ducks' heads. The Egyptians, shown in more maneuverable ships manned by rowers and bristling with bowmen, appear to have trapped the invaders against the shore, most likely in one of the mouths of the Nile. More bowmen line the riverbanks, pouring arrows into any enemy ship that drifts within range. Other enemy vessels are shown capsized or in the process of being rammed by the Egyptian ships or snared with grappling hooks. Drowning men fill the water, and these, according to the inscription, were later "dragged, hemmed in, prostrated on the beach, and made into heaps." Beneath the battle scene those enemy warriors who survived the lopsided melee are depicted being led away into slavery, their hands and arms "pinioned like birds" *(page 127)*.

In the aftermath of the battle, Ramses III displayed understandable pride in his triumph over the Sea Peoples. In the Great Harris Papyrus he boasts, "I extended all the frontiers of Egypt and overthrew those who had attacked them from their lands. I slew the Denyen in their islands, while the Tjekker and the Peleset were made ashes. The Sherden and the Weshesh of the Sea were made non-existent, taken captive all together and brought in captivity to Egypt like the sands of the shore."

The subjugation of the Sea Peoples hardly ended Ramses III's exploits on the battlefield. Just three years later, in year 11 of the pharaoh's reign, the Libyans were back, again in league with the Meshwesh and their chieftain Mesher. Surging eastward across the delta, the attackers apparently got as far as a canal called the Water of Re. There they were met and crushed by Ramses and his forces, who killed more than 2,000 of the enemy and captured as many more, including Mesher himself. Another relief at Medinet Habu shows the chieftain's father, Keper, pleading with Ramses to spare his son's life. Showing no mercy, the pharaoh had the son executed on the spot, then, for good measure, ordered the father killed as well.

Elsewhere at Medinet Habu, Ramses III is shown invading Syria, Hatti, and Amurru. Some scholars question whether these scenes have any basis in fact since Hatti and Amurru had ceased to exist as political entities by this time. They suspect that the carvings are merely copies of similar battle reliefs commissioned by Ramses II. Ramses III in fact blatantly modeled himself on his famous predecessor, even naming his children and horses after those of Ramses II.

Ramses III's military adventures were, in any case, mostly over by the 12th year of his reign. He was able to turn his attention to the home front, confident that he had reduced foreign threats and restored peace throughout his realm. "I planted the whole land with trees and verdure, and I let the people sit in their shade," Ramses can be heard bragging in the Great Harris Papyrus. "I caused the woman of Egypt to travel freely to the place where she would go, for no foreigner or anyone on the road molested her."

With peace came a period of prosperity that would last until the latter years of the pharaoh's reign and would find its most exalted expression in the temple complex at Medinet Habu, home to the reliefs that form such a vivid record of Ramses III's reign. Here, behind a wall more than half a mile long and 60 feet high, Ramses erected a monument to his own ambition that was at once a temple, palace, and fortress. Here, too, carvings on one of the surviving interior walls of an unusual multistoried gateway offer an intimate glimpse of palace life, with the pharaoh attended by the women of his harem and quite obviously enjoying the pleasure of their company.

Despite appearances, however, all was not well in the world beyond the walls of Medinet Habu. In fact, not far away, in Deir el Medina, the royal tomb workers were increasingly frustrated by the delays in the routine delivery of the rations that constituted their pay. Finally, on November 14 of year 29 of Ramses III's reign, after their repeated requests for relief had gone unheeded by authorities, the workers walked off the job—the first recorded strike in history and only the first of a number of stoppages they would stage in the months ahead.

Curiously, there was no shortage of food at the time; on

In this detail of a relief at Medinet Habu, a scribe drops severed human hands, one from each enemy soldier killed during Ramses III's second Libyan war, into a heap for tallying. Accompanying inscriptions say the pharaoh's victorious troops gathered 2,175 such grisly trophies.

the contrary, the temple granaries were full. Rather, a combination of administrative inefficiency and outright corruption had led to a breakdown in the distribution of food, including the rations of the royal tomb makers. At the same time, with the pharaoh and court resident in Memphis, once mighty Thebes had increasingly become a political backwater, isolated from its king, its needs now neglected, its complaints frequently ignored.

Indeed, even as his tomb makers continued to starve and strike, Ramses III concentrated on his own upcoming jubilee, or Heb-Sed. No mere festival, the Heb-Sed was a series of rituals dating back to the earliest dynasties that was believed to renew the powers of the reigning king. Typically, a king's first jubilee would be held after 30 years on the throne, with subsequent jubilees at random intervals thereafter. Ramses II, for example, may have celebrated his 14th Heb-Sed before he died, an achievement his admiring successor no doubt hoped to duplicate.

But, as a number of judicial papyri make clear, Ramses III would not be so fortunate. Those documents detail a plot—hatched in the king's own harem by a minor queen eager to put her son on the throne—to assassinate the pharaoh on the first day of Ramses' 32nd year on the throne. Eventually, at least 28 other people were drawn into the conspiracy, including government officials, an army commander, and three royal scribes. The culprits were arrested, perhaps after actually attempting to kill the king, though this is not entirely certain, then tried by a panel of 12 judges who had been appointed by the pharaoh himself. Most of the accused were either executed or condemned to suicide.

The same papyri also tell of a surprising turn of events that took place sometime during the trial. In what can be read as a sign of the moral decay of the time, five of the judges openly caroused with some of the female conspirators. For his lack of judicial restraint, one received a reprimand. The others paid more dearly for their indiscretion, with one magistrate sentenced to commit suicide and the others summarily relieved of their noses and ears.

For all their sometimes gory detail, however, the texts do not disclose whether the plot against the king succeeded. What is known is that several weeks after the attempt on his life, Ramses III died, the date of his passing carefully noted by a scribe to the royal tomb makers, along with the traditional acknowledgment of a king's death, "The Falcon has flown up to Heaven." Whether his death came as a

BEHIND THICK PROTECTIVE WALLS, A PLACE OF DEATH DESIGNED FOR PLEASURE

When the University of Chicago's Oriental Institute epigraphers started the painstaking work of recording the reliefs and inscriptions of Ramses III's temple at Medinet Habu in 1924, archaeology had succeeded in unveiling few of the site's architectural secrets. Auguste Mariette, the famed French Egyptologist, had cleared rubble from around a tower gate standing to the east of the temple in the late 1850s *(right),* and the archaeologist-photographer Harry Burton had revealed remains of what appeared to be a palace—pieces of columns, thresholds of doorways, and the base of a throne —immediately to the south in 1912. Yet the exact nature of these structures remained a mystery until 1927, when the Oriental Institute organized a team of archaeologists, engineers, and other experts to survey the entire precinct.

The evidence the group uncovered suggests that the complex—originally no more than the temple, a small palace, and storerooms, all ringed by a single wall—was transformed into the fortresslike complex shown below during the second half of Ramses III's reign. The palace was razed and rebuilt, and two outer walls were added.

The renovations lent the site an imposing, martial look, yet archaeologists believe domestic considerations played as big a role in the work as fears of attack. The new palace contained a six-columned audience hall, three alabaster thrones, four sets of baths, toilets, and dressing rooms, a royal bedroom, in which the raised bed was reached by climbing a short flight of steps, and a harem. Thus on visits to his mortuary temple, perhaps with thoughts of his death in mind, Ramses III could still avail himself of the pleasures life had to offer.

Ramses III's temple and second palace at Medinet Habu nestled within three protective rings: an inner wall, the Great Girdle Wall, and an outer wall. The quay at the bottom linked the complex with a canal that led to the Nile.

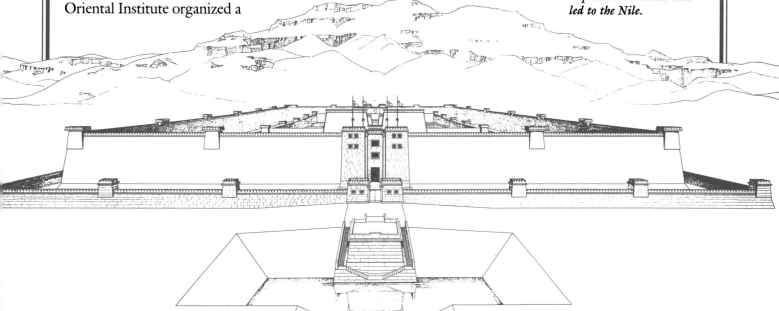

result of the attempted coup d'état or of natural causes is open to conjecture, although his mummy in the Egyptian Museum in Cairo bears no signs of foul play.

Ramses III's son now assumed the throne, and it was shortly thereafter that the new pharaoh compiled the Great Harris Papyrus. Dated on the day of the death of Ramses III, the papyrus at one point expresses the father's hope that his son would enjoy a long reign and would "triumph for Egypt as sovereign of the two lands." Four years into his own reign, Ramses IV said as much himself, when, in a prayer found chiseled onto a huge limestone stele at Abydos, the pharaoh begged the god Osiris to grant him a reign twice as long as that of Ramses II.

The pharaoh's prayer apparently went unanswered, since a later papyrus indicates that instead of the 134 years he had asked for, Ramses IV reigned no longer than 6. During that time, however, the pharaoh undertook an ambitious building program that might have been the envy of the equally enterprising Ramses II. Part of this program was Ramses IV's own tomb, whose plan—one of only two royal tomb plans known to have survived—is preserved on a papyrus in the Egyptian Museum in Turin, Italy. In addition, the king began work on two large temples in western Thebes, one of which took its inspiration from his father's vast temple at Medinet Habu but was half again as large. It survives today only as the ghost of a foundation near Deir el Bahri. Other temples planned for Memphis and Abydos barely got beyond the drawing-board stage, while a much smaller mortuary temple was actually completed in western Thebes.

To provide the stone for these projects, Ramses IV reopened the quarries in the Wadi Hammamat, some 70 miles from Thebes. It was probably during this time that a papyrus map—the world's oldest surviving map, also in Turin's Egyptian Museum—was completed. A number of expeditions to the site were mounted in order to extract graywacke, a stone similar to slate. These expeditions are chronicled in the rock of the Wadi Hammamat itself, both in hieroglyphs inscribed by the royal sculptors and in graffiti scratched into the cliffs by the workers. During the largest of the expeditions, more

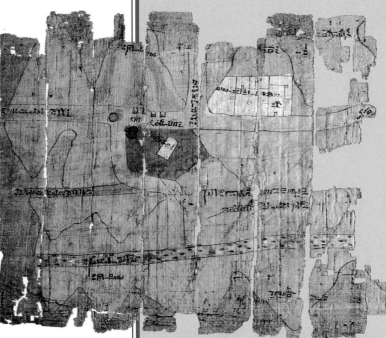

The fragment of papyrus reproduced above is part of the world's oldest geologic map and its second oldest geographical one as well. In all likelihood it belonged to a scribe in the tomb-workers community of Deir el Medina close by the Valley of the Kings. Probably drawn during the reign of Ramses IV, it records a site called Wadi Hammamat today, famous in ancient times for its gold mines and slatelike, grayish green rock—graywacke—from which the kneeling figure of the pharaoh at right was carved. Ramses IV is known to have dispatched at least three quarrying expeditions to the area; the third, which included more than 8,000 men, was intended to obtain stone for his mortuary temple and other monuments.

The map seems to have lain forgotten in a tomb—perhaps that

of the scribe who drew it—until graverobbers found it and sold it, via intermediaries, to an Italian collector in the early part of the 19th century. Measuring 16 inches wide and perhaps once as long as 9 feet, it exists today only in sections. Visible in the fragment are hills, the Wadi Hammamat *(foreground)*, a dry riverbed that served as a road, four goldminers' houses, and a shrine to Amen. The brown bands on the slope behind the houses represent gold-bearing veins of quartz.

Holding pots of wine, Ramses IV makes an offering to a god. Of his quarrying expeditions to Wadi Hammamat, only this much restored statue and one other of him carved from stone obtained there survive as mementos of his desire to immortalize himself on a grandiose scale.

than 8,000 men—including 2,000 soldiers—under the supervision of the high priest of Amen at Karnak, labored under unspeakably harsh conditions in the desert. Many of the men had to drag huge blocks, some weighing 40 tons or more, the 60-odd miles to the Nile, where the stones were loaded aboard rafts for the trip to Thebes. Not surprisingly, the death toll was staggering; some 900 of the workers never left the desert alive.

In spite of all the effort expended and the hardship endured, by the time Ramses IV died around 1160 BC, little had actually been accomplished—even his own tomb lay incomplete. In Ramses IV's wake came a procession of seven kings, all of them called Ramses, most of whom departed in short order and did little more than preside over Egypt's continuing decline.

An empire now only in name, Egypt suffered repeatedly during this period from a series of low Nile floods. The resulting lean harvests, growing food shortages, and rising inflation all helped to fuel unrest at home. Conditions were further exacerbated by the administrative inefficiency and corruption evident during the last years of the reign of Ramses III that had since become endemic. In one of the most glaring examples of this corruption, an indictment papyrus from the reign of Ramses V tells of a group of officials who had siphoned off nearly all of the grain revenues from one small temple at Elephantine Island—enough grain to provide four months' rations for the royal tomb makers at Deir el Medina, about 140 miles to the north. Worse still, those officials had gotten away with their crimes for a decade, doubtless while authorities turned a blind eye.

Indeed, back in Memphis, diffidence reigned as mightily as any one pharaoh. Showing less and less interest in day-to-day governmental proceedings, the pharaohs entrusted the nation's well-being to a bureaucracy that was itself increasingly hereditary in nature. To make matters worse, the kings cut back on their tours of the country. The power vacuum was particularly acute in the southern half of the realm, where even the office of vizier—one of Egypt's two chief administrators—had been abolished. Now there was often only one vizier, who, like the pharaoh, spent most of his time some 400 miles down the Nile in the capital.

As the influence of the kings waned, especially in Upper Egypt, the high priests of Amen gradually exerted greater authority in the region. During the time of Ramses III, Karnak had become wealthier—the king lavishly donated to the temples over a period of more than 30 years—and more powerful than before. From the Great Harris Papyrus, which lists numerous endowments, scholars have estimated that about one-third of all arable land in the country now belonged to religious institutions, some three-quarters of that property to the Temple of Amen alone.

A powerful family—headed by Merybast, Ramses III's chief tax master and steward of the king's mortuary temple at Medinet Habu—emerged in the venerable city of Thebes. The position of high priest went to Merybast's son Ramsesnakht, who may have succeeded a brother in that capacity. Ramsesnakht served under at least three pharaohs, Ramses IV, V, and VI, before passing on the high priesthood to his own sons. Another offspring became the steward of Amen, administrator of royal lands, and chief tax master, positions that were once held by his grandfather. The wealth of the chief god's estates and the finances of the royal domains were thus firmly in the hands of a single family.

Under Ramsesnakht, the high priesthood seems to have acquired new rights and responsibilities in the wake of the tomb workers' strikes at Deir el Medina. Acting as intermediary between the pharaoh and the royal work force, the high priest soon took part in the distribution of the villagers' rations, probably supplementing their wages from temple funds. Ramsesnakht had also led the great expedition to the stone quarries in the Wadi Hammamat and attended work in the Valley of the Kings.

When Ramsesnakht's son Amenhotep became high priest, he wielded such authority that by the time of Ramses IX, he could take the unprecedented step of having himself depicted on the wall of the temple at Karnak as an equal in stature to the pharaoh himself. But in the unsettled political climate of the time, even the high priests had little influence over the course of events in Memphis.

A daily log of events at Deir el Medina kept during the reign of Ramses V or Ramses VI by one of the scribes assigned to the king's tomb notes that the workers had been "idle from fear of the enemy." Still another entry records a rumor that the same unspecified enemy had attacked a town to the north of Thebes, destroying everything and burning its people, and further states that the high priest of Amen had ordered the police to stand guard at the tombs. A few days later, the tomb makers were told not to report to work in the Valley of the Kings at all. "Do not go up until you see what has happened," the local chief of police is reported as saying. "I will go to have a look for you and to hear what they say, and I myself will come to tell you to go up." Just who the enemy was remains uncertain, but some scholars are convinced that the threat came from Libyan marauders and Egyptian bandits active in the area.

Ramses VI had a reign of a little over seven years, making way for Ramses VII and Ramses VIII. Conditions in Egypt continued to deteriorate during their reigns, as inflation drove up the prices of grain and drove down the standard of living. In fact, by the fourth year of Ramses VII, grain prices, as reflected in a contemporary papyrus, had risen to three times their preinflationary levels.

There was still worse to come. Sometime between years 10 and 15 of Ramses IX's reign, Libyans began launching a number of incursions into Egypt that would eventually bring them as far as Thebes. A fragmentary report from the period records that "desert-dwellers," identified elsewhere in the papyrus as the Libyans' old allies the Meshwesh, had descended on the area, causing the tomb makers to abandon their work and take refuge within the walls of Deir el Medina. Other journals, from year 15 of Ramses IX's reign and as late as year 3 of his successor's, tell of similar encroachments by the Libyans. But unlike the glory days of the New Kingdom, when both Merenptah and Ramses III had dealt severely and successfully with Libyan invaders, these incursions seem to have provoked no response from the Egyptian government. Rather, the evidence appears to suggest that the Egyptians, either unwilling or unable to put a stop to the infiltration, had simply put the Libyans on the royal payroll as mercenaries.

In the meantime, year after year of low Nile floods and poor harvests, combined with the usual bureaucratic inefficiency and graft, had finally resulted in famine. Work at the royal tombs came to a standstill, as the artisans, deprived now of their monthly grain rations, again walked off the job. Some of the laborers, desperate for any source of additional income that would allow them to barter for food, seem to have taken to plundering the private cemeteries that surrounded their village.

Other gangs of tomb robbers, who had been despoiling Theban graves for years, were now roaming up and down the Nile, looting tombs all along the river. The authorities responded by step-

Rectangular entrances to royal tombs line the footpaths that crisscross the main branch of the Valley of the Kings, just north of 600-foot-tall el Qurn seen at the center. The peak's strong pyramidal shape may have been the reason why the area became a focus for burials. About a mile to the southeast, Medinet Habu, its long north wall bathed in morning light, is visible at upper left.

ping up their inspections of the graves and by keeping an even more watchful eye on the tombs of the kings. The inspectors, however, were usually satisfied to find the tombs' doors still intact and their seals unbroken, while the looters invariably entered a vault by tunneling in from the rear. In those rare instances when someone was actually arrested and accused of tomb robbing, the miscreant could frequently bribe his way out of jail simply by sharing some of his booty with the proper officials.

It was only a matter of time before the thieves, many of whom operated in organized teams whose members had specific tasks, turned their attention to even richer hoards, the tombs of Egypt's kings and queens. By then, so many government and temple officials—the very people charged with protecting the tombs—were in the pockets of the thieves that for all intents and purposes the burglaries were officially sanctioned.

Not until year 16 of the reign of Ramses IX was a commission appointed to look into the growing number of rumors that the royal tombs had been violated. Its investigation resulted in the arrest and conviction of a handful of scapegoats and a speedy return to the business of thievery as usual.

The following year, however, Amenhotep, now the high priest of Amen, and the mayor of Thebes redoubled efforts to prove the widespread suspicions that some of the royal tomb makers themselves were behind the thievery. Eight of the artisans were subsequently charged with tomb robbery, and documents from the time reveal that the eight men had been found in possession of treasures stolen from the tomb of Queen Isis, the wife of Ramses III. The beating and limb twisting that constituted official questioning resulted in the inevitable confessions, although the fate of the culprits remains unknown.

Ominously, the men's names never appear again in village records, and the words of another accused tomb robber, some 30 years later, provide a further clue that the eight thieves paid for their crime with their lives: "I saw the punishment that was inflicted upon the thieves in the time of the Vizier Khaemwase. Is it likely then that I would risk incurring such a death?"

This robbery, like the many others that had

OLD COFFINS PUT TO NEW USES

In 1940, when French Egyptologist Pierre Montet excavated the tomb of Psusennes I, pharaoh from 1040 to 992 BC, in the delta, he found the ruler's coffins in a recycled red granite sarcophagus that once belonged to Merenptah, 13th son of Ramses II and pharaoh from 1224 to 1214 BC. Every cartouche on the casket identifying the earlier leader had been hastily carved over to read Psusennes I, and only one sign on the lid—on the belt buckle of the mummiform figure that adorns it—had been left unaltered. Clearly, Merenptah's grave in the Valley of the Kings had been plundered, apparently with official permission, yet how remained unclear until Edwin Brock, director of the Canadian Institute in Egypt, picked through the burial site in the late 1980s.

Inside the tomb, Brock discovered that the sarcophagus found by Montet originally nested within two larger ones, also made of red

granite. Though the lids of these had survived, few traces of the boxes themselves remained. About a third of the rectangular outer case (*pictured below, left*) and a fifth of the cartouche-shaped second coffin could be pieced together. They and a small fourth or innermost sarcophagus—a fragment of which resides in the British Museum—had been smashed. Brock theorized that their thick granite bases were split into slabs and recycled and only the third coffin—Montet's find—emerged from the tomb intact. The single obstacle the trespassers had to overcome in removing it was a 17-foot-deep pit, symbolizing the underworld, located about midway between the tomb's inner chambers and the entrance. They simply filled it in with the debris left from the tomb's construction. Brock's excavation of the pit revealed marks on the edge, made when the intruders dumped in the rubble.

Inside Merenptah's tomb, the outermost of his red granite sarcophagi (left) *lies in fragments, shattered in ancient times by scavengers who recycled its bottom slab. To salvage the stone, the intruders first had to fill in a deep shaft such as the one above, located in the tomb of Ramses XI, then drag the reclaimed blocks across.*

so far gone undetected, generated gold, silver, and copper, as well as jewelry, linens, precious oils, and furniture. Some of the loot became the thieves' own household possessions, but more of it flowed back into the economy, where it was bartered for goods and services. Indeed, the confessions wrested from the eight thieves revealed that between outright bribes and payments for various goods and services, the proceeds from tomb robbery were percolating into virtually every layer of Theban society.

The death of Ramses IX, after some 18 years on the throne, and the accession of a new Ramses in 1109 BC did nothing to slow down the traffic in stolen grave goods. Moreover, under Ramses X the country continued to experience serious food shortages, which were aggravated even further now by a drought in lower Nubia. Early in the reign of Ramses XI—a time so terrible that one year in particular would later be remembered as the Year of the Hyenas—the situation in Egypt bordered on anarchy.

Tomb robbery was rife, and the temples became the targets of gangs of brazen looters who roamed Thebes, breaking into the buildings and stripping them of their treasures. More than 80 pounds of gold and silver were ripped from the doorways of the temple of Ramses II alone. Even the priests and other temple officials participated in the thievery, helping themselves to whatever could easily be removed.

The high priest of Amen, Amenhotep, his authority now all but gone, appealed to the king for assistance. But instead of sending troops south from the delta, Ramses XI ordered Panehesy, the viceroy of Nubia, to move his forces north. The viceroy acted quickly to restore order in Thebes and soon ordered an investigation of the tomb and temple robberies, although not before his own Nubian troops had joined in the looting. Panehesy also seems to have temporarily relieved Amenhotep of his duties, according to one papyrus, which notes a nine-month suppression of the high priest. Another papyrus pointedly refers to this period as "the war of the high priest."

Although Amenhotep was later reinstated on orders from Ramses XI, Panehesy retained administrative control of Upper Egypt for himself and seems to have ruled without much interference from the king for the next several years. Even as late as year 17

of the reign of Ramses XI, a taxation papyrus and a letter from the pharaoh's chancellery indicate that Panehesy was still at the helm in Thebes. By year 19, however, Panehesy had become an enemy of the state, and his name is thereafter always associated with a hieroglyph that means "enemy" or "death."

The circumstances of Panehesy's fall from grace are uncertain, but it appears that at some point he retreated to Nubia. In his place a general named Herihor assumed control, not only as commander of the army but also as high priest of Amen and viceroy of Nubia—the first time in Egyptian history that all three titles had been vested in one person. To these he added the office of vizier of Upper Egypt. An ostracon further identifies Herihor as "Captain at the Head of the Army of All Egypt," and it was this title, along with the high priesthood, that his descendants would inherit.

Such was the power wielded by Herihor that within a few years he would outdo even Amenhotep, the erstwhile high priest, by brazenly having himself depicted as pharaoh—both in name and in dress—on the walls of the forecourt of the Temple of Khonsu at Karnak, even going so far in one cartouche as to claim divine descent. Later still, his son-in-law and heir, Piankh, would match his own authority against that of Ramses XI and ask contemptuously in a letter, "Of whom is Pharaoh superior still?"

Herihor's pretensions to power and Piankh's effrontery notwithstanding, Ramses XI did reign supreme as pharaoh, and Herihor's kingship never really extended beyond the walls of the Temple of Khonsu. Indeed, with the government of Upper Egypt in the good hands of Herihor, the king felt confident enough in the 19th year of his reign to proclaim a renaissance—literally a "repeating-of-birth"—in effect turning back the clock on the remaining years of his reign. Thus, year 19 became year 1 of the renaissance. Coincidentally, order and prosperity returned to Egypt, at least temporarily, as the Nile floods returned to normal levels. Even the economy was improving, thanks largely to the infusion of stolen grave goods, which, in the marketplace, had the positive effect of stemming inflation and reducing grain prices.

Having decreed a new era, Ramses XI now decided to clean up some old business. He ordered a thorough investigation into the plunder of the tombs and temples of Thebes some 10 years earlier during the Year of the Hyenas. A

The two cartouches and script inked on this cedar coffin lid state that it belongs to Ramses II. The coffin, dating from the 18th Dynasty, was a substitute for the one in which the pharaoh was entombed; the valuable original was probably stolen by graverobbers.

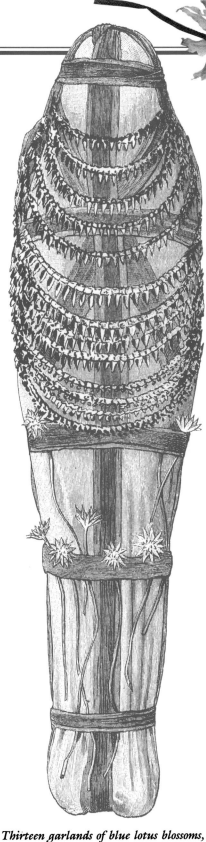

Thirteen garlands of blue lotus blossoms, one of which is shown at top, adorn a mummy in this sketch made after the discovery in 1881 of 40 bodies in a well-hidden tomb. One who saw such flowers on the mummies before the wrappings were unwound said they presented the "image of endless sleep."

commission was appointed by the king, consisting of members of the royal court, and it quickly began gathering evidence and statements from witnesses.

Most of the evidence has not survived, but the witnesses' statements did come to light in 1850 when two jars, each of them containing several rolls of papyri, were unearthed. For a number of years afterward, the papyri were repeatedly bought and sold before finally coming to rest in a number of museums. There, many of the texts were consigned to storerooms after their hieratic script proved to be too stubborn for interpretation, and there they stayed awaiting later generations of Egyptologists with the knowledge necessary to translate them.

It was a young Englishman, T. Eric Peet, who was finally able to decipher the papyri, two of which were published in 1920. A decade later, just four years before his own untimely death in 1934, Peet completed his studies and published the results in *The Great Tomb-Robberies of the Twentieth Egyptian Dynasty*.

As translated by Peet, the papyri revealed that the commission took statements from members of all levels of Theban society. More than 100 suspected thieves were arrested, as were the wives of those suspects who had had the audacity to die in the years since they had committed their crimes. All were questioned, and some were subjected to more rigorous examination using the standard means of persuasion, "the birch, the stick, and the screw." Not surprisingly, many of them readily confessed.

The surviving documents also revealed that the inquisitors had frequently been able to ascertain the fate of the loot, some of which had actually been recovered during the initial investigation conducted by Panehesy a decade earlier. In some instances, the stolen items were small, such as the modest amount of metal discovered in the possession of a workman's wife, although even such insignificant items had value in the thriving black market of the time. Another woman denied having used stolen silver to buy servants and instead tried to convince the commission that she had paid for the servants with dates that had been gathered from her palm grove. Still another one claimed that the silver in her possession had not been stolen at all but had been received "in exchange for barley in the year of the hyenas, when there was a famine."

Upon questioning, other thieves admitted trading booty for everything from honey to slaves to land. A few of the accused used their loot to pay off debts, while others, such as one thief who apparently boasted of his exploits within earshot of the scribe of the royal records, made a different kind of payoff. When the scribe threatened to report what he had heard to the high priest of Amen, the thief did what any other thief might have done in the same situation: "So we brought 3 *kite* of gold and gave it to the scribe of the royal records, Setekhmes."

The death of Ramses XI in 1070 BC not only brought the renaissance and the 20th Dynasty to a close but also marked the end of the New Kingdom. With no surviving sons of the royal bloodline and with the powerful Herihor already in his grave, it was left to Smendes—who had governed Lower Egypt under the dead pharaoh as Herihor had governed Upper Egypt—to establish a new dynasty over what remained of Ramses II's once splendid empire.

By all accounts, Ramses XI had reigned for at least 28 years, and in accordance with the architectural tradition that each king's tomb should be about five percent bigger than that of his predecessor, this pharaoh's was the largest ever planned. At his death, however, Ramses XI's tomb remained unfinished and was, in any case, destined never to be occupied by the dead pharaoh. Having spent so much of his reign in Memphis, he would now spend eternity close to home, in Saqqara, where his mummy could be better guarded.

Indeed, the looting of the royal tombs had shown that the Valley of the Kings could no longer be considered inviolate. Already, nearly all of the tombs there had been entered and robbed, most of them in the years since the death of Ramses III, and some, perhaps, before the tombs had even been sealed. Others, from the 18th Dynasty, were found to have been plundered centuries before. Under Herihor and his successors, the royal mummies were gathered for restoration and reburial.

The actual repairs took place in the unfinished tomb of Ramses XI. There, the plundered mummies, some of which had been dismembered in the robbers' haste to strip them of their jewels and amulets, were carefully pieced back together and ritually rewrapped. At the same time, in what can be viewed as yet one more insult to the sacred dead, any treasures that the robbers had overlooked—whether inside the tombs or within the mummies' wrappings—were now quietly pilfered by the priests who were conducting the restorations. Even the gold foil found on many of the coffins was carefully scraped

FACE TO FACE WITH SOME OF EGYPT'S GREATEST PHARAOHS

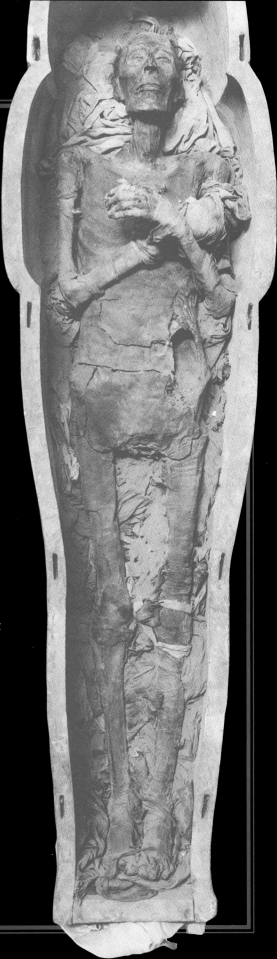

With the discovery, toward the end of the 19th century, of two secret caches of mummies from the 17th through the 21st dynasties, the impossible suddenly became possible: People of the modern world could gaze upon the faces of some of the greatest movers and shakers of the ancient world. "I ask myself if I am not dreaming when I see and touch the bodies of so many rulers," said an awed Gaston Maspero, who was among the first to enter the chamber where 40 mummies had been hidden almost 3,000 years earlier by priests seeking to safeguard them from graverobbers. And among those he beheld—some of them damaged by the plunderers who had torn through their wrappings and hacked away at their bodies to obtain concealed valuables—was none other than that of Ramses II, seen preserved in a wooden coffin in the photograph at right.

The eerie picture was taken in the early part of the 20th century by the British anatomist Sir Grafton Elliot Smith as part of a remarkable series he made of the royal mummies in the Egyptian Museum in Cairo *(overleaf)*. In addition to photographing the bodies in detail, he examined them forensically and published his findings in a 1912 mono-

graph. Fortunately, Smith approached his task with scientific integrity, using no invasive techniques that might have harmed these fragile voyagers from times past. He refused to investigate internally any that were "encased," as he put it, "in a resinous carapace," the caked and hardened coat applied by the embalmers; to have removed it might have caused irreparable damage.

Smith's studies revealed a wealth of personal and sometime startling detail—Ramses II, for example, had blackheads—as well as information about the illnesses and ailments that had afflicted the pharaohs and even, in some instances, had brought about their deaths.

To his critics, who thought such giants of the past should not undergo "anthropological investigations" or be seen naked once they were unwrapped, Smith had a ready answer: "Those who make such complaints seem to be unaware that the real desecration was committed 29 centuries ago by the subjects of these rulers."

Hands across his chest, Ramses II is coated with the resin used in the mummification process. The hole in his abdomen was enlarged by graverobbers seeking treasures hidden in the body cavity from which the embalmers had removed the organs.

19TH DYNASTY

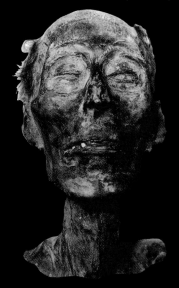

SETI I
When unwrapped, Seti's skin turned from brown to black. His body, stuffed with resin-soaked linen, still contained his petrified, jet-black heart.

RAMSES II
Its wrinkles smoothed by the embalmers, Ramses' face has whiskers around the lips and on the chin. Like most New Kingdom pharaohs, he has pierced ears.

MERENPTAH
A layer of salt covered the body of Ramses' son. He was fat, as revealed by what Smith called a "redundancy" of skin on his belly, thighs, and cheeks.

SETI II
Seti II's head was broken off by graverobbers looting his tomb but still displays a delicate acquiline nose. He has protruding upper teeth.

SIPTAH
Graverobbers damaged the face of Siptah and broke his right arm, which was repaired with splints by priests. He showed evidence of having had polio.

20TH DYNASTY

RAMSES III
Recipient of 20th-Dynasty embalming innovations, Ramses III was given artificial eyeballs of stone, and his lids were puffed up with linen backing.

RAMSES IV
Ramses IV had onions substituted for eyes. "The light brown color of the dried onion distending the eyelids lends quite a natural appearance," wrote Smith.

RAMSES V
His face painted an earthy red, Ramses V still exhibits the pustules that covered it, as well as his abdomen. He probably died of small pox.

RAMSES VI
The body of Ramses VI was in such poor condition after graverobbers finished with it that the pieces had to be strapped to a board by the priests.

away, leaving only the royal names and titles on some of them.

Most of the mummies were never returned to their original tombs. Instead, in an effort to prevent the dead kings from ever being desecrated again, the priests began an elaborate shell game that saw the mummies moved from tomb to tomb over a number of decades. Hieratic notes jotted down by the priests and later found with the royal bodies chronicle both the restorations and relocations.

The mummy of Ramses II, for example, was temporarily stored in the tomb of his father, Seti I. Years later, during the reign of Siamun, one of the last of the 21st-Dynasty kings, it was moved again. This time, the mummy was lowered into the ancient rock tomb of Queen Inhapy, lying below the cliffs in a small valley south of Deir el Bahri, where it joined some 40 other mummies in a place that seemed to offer the most security.

Nine other kings, as well as one queen and a number of princes, were similarly collected and stowed in a second cache—the tomb of Amenhotep II in the Valley of the Kings. For the next 2,800 years, the mummies in these two royal repositories lay exactly as the priests had left them back in the 10th century BC. In 1898 the tomb of Amenhotep II and its hidden hoard of monarchs was finally found—accidentally—when the French archaeologist Victor Loret stumbled upon it in the course of exploring another tomb. Deep in the second tomb, Loret could only stare in amazement as his candle spread light across the coffins of such New Kingdom monarchs as Siptah, Seti II, Merenptah, and Ramses IV, V, and VI.

A similar twist of fate in the early 1870s had brought to light the final resting place of Ramses II at Deir el Bahri. It is a story often told. A goatherd, supposedly looking for a missing kid, spotted the animal at the bottom of what appeared to be only a deep hole. As the goatherd soon discovered, however, that particular hole led to a doorway, which in turn led to a series of corridors that opened into a chamber that was piled high with coffins.

The goatherd kept his secret for the next 10 years, sharing it with only a few family members, who then used the tomb as a private treasure trove until an older brother finally tipped off the authorities. Within days the tomb was hurriedly emptied of its contents by archaeologists eager to keep one of the most important finds in Egyptian history out of the hands of local villagers.

By June of 1886 the mummy of Ramses II was the guest

of honor at the Egyptian Museum in Cairo. There, in front of the assembled dignitaries, the French archaeologist Gaston Maspero, the director-general of the Egyptian Antiquities Service, pointed out the three inscriptions on the king's coffin. The first of these inscriptions described how the mummy had been restored at the request of Herihor; the other two recounted the mummy's subsequent transfers, first from its original resting place to the tomb of Seti I and later to the tomb of Queen Inhapy.

The director-general next loosened the wrappings that covered the mummy's chest, opening them just enough to allow a hieratic inscription on the shroud to peek through. Translated, this inscription confirmed that the corpse was indeed Ramses II. Only then did the unwrapping resume, this time in earnest. Less than 15 minutes later, the world was again face-to-face with the king whose exploits both at home and on the battlefield had caused 19th-century Egyptologists to dub him "the Great."

Once unwrapped, Ramses' mummy was found to be almost perfectly preserved. The same could not be said for one of the king's tomb mates, Queen Ahmose Nefertari, the mother of Amenhotep I. By the time it was finally divested of bandages, this mummy was found to be rapidly decomposing. To rid the corpse of its awful smell, it was buried for a few months beneath the museum's storehouse.

An anonymous New Kingdom mummy known as Lady X is used in a tryout of a prototype display case specially developed by the Getty Conservation Institute. Designed to house some of the Egyptian Museum in Cairo's royal mummies, the airtight cabinet automatically regulates temperature and humidity and contains less than two percent oxygen, to hinder the growth of microorganisms.

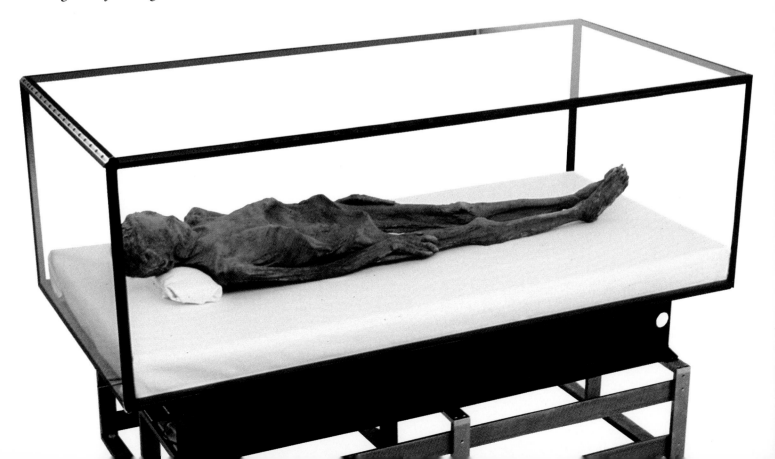

Eventually, Ramses II and other royal mummies were housed in a special room at the museum, each in its own coffin within a display case whose glass cover could be slid away to allow museum officials or attendants armed with old-fashioned spray guns to douse the corpse with insecticide. For Ramses II, such treatment was a far cry from those long-ago days when the very air around him was scented with the sacred fragrances reserved for the pleasure of the god-king, the bouquet continuously and ceremoniously wafted through the air by fan bearers.

Nor have these periodic treatments with toxic chemicals been the least of the indignities the dead king has had to endure. In the century since its rediscovery, the mummy has been displayed for a time in a standing position, dipped in mercury to kill lice, examined and reexamined, x-rayed, probed with an endoscope, and even flown to Paris in 1976 for further tests and restoration.

At the beginning of the 20th century, Ramses II's mummy had been studied and photographed by the British scientist Sir Grafton Elliot Smith. The great pharaoh's own comment on all of the attention he has received may well have come when one of Elliot Smith's assistants unwrapped the mummy yet again. The long-compressed fibers in the royal arm suddenly retracted. The scientists who were clustered next to the corpse sprang back in alarm as the dead king, seemingly roused from his endless sleep, unexpectedly gestured, as though he would once again issue an order to those around him. "Certainly," in the words of archaeologist John Romer, "if he could speak, the ancient king would command a return to the quiet Theban Hills."

RAMSES IN PARIS

On September 26, 1976, Ramses the Great—warrior, master diplomat, prolific builder, and god—became the first pharaoh ever to travel by airplane. Protected from turbulence by a sturdy wood case labeled with the words *haut* and *bas (above)*, French for top and bottom, the pharaoh rested in a modern oak coffin, his desiccated head, arms, and legs cushioned by layers of tissue paper, cotton, and foam rubber. His immediate destination lay across the Mediterranean: the airport at Le Bourget, France, a suburb of Paris, where Charles Lindbergh had put down after his epoch transoceanic flight almost 50 years earlier.

The motivation for the sojourn was the imperiled condition of the mummy. Grafton Elliot Smith's photographs *(page 143)* showed that Ramses' evisceration orifice, the opening through which embalmers had removed his inner organs and which had been enlarged by tomb robbers, was already gaping as early as 1912. But the obvious deterioration of the mummy since then alarmed Egyptian and French scientists who studied it in Cairo in the early 1970s. A network of cracks, they found, now ran along the resinous shield covering his arms and legs and across his chest and abdomen. The most alarming of these, a jagged 14-inch-long tear, stretched from hip to hip. Worse, upon opening Ramses' glass display case, the investigators were assaulted by a rank odor that led them to suspect bacteria were growing on or inside the mummy. The scientists also detected pale-colored fungi, samples of which they examined under a microscope. Clearly, intervention would be required.

After lengthy negotiations, it was agreed to transport the mummy to the French capital for almost eight months of study and conservation. As shown on the following pages, the services of more than 40 laboratories and a battery of advanced diagnostic tools were put at the investigators' disposal. The extraordinary results greatly enlarged knowledge of Ramses, the man.

FIRST-CLASS CARE FOR AN ANCIENT VISITOR

In Paris, Ramses took up residence on the third floor of the Museum of Man, located in one of the city's most elegant neighborhoods, where two rooms—an examination area and a so-called bedroom—had been specially constructed for him. Air-conditioning units in each chamber kept the temperature and relative humidity low enough to curtail further growth of fungi, and a silvery blue film applied to the windows blocked out all harmful ultraviolet radiation. Laboratory attendants monitored the ruler's environment daily, and guards stood watch night and day to keep out unauthorized visitors.

Concerns about the extreme fragility of the mummy dictated that it never be moved outside the museum and that it be transported from bedroom to workroom only if the temperature and humidity in each chamber were equal. The scientists did not risk lifting the body. Instead, they sawed off the foot end of the oak coffin in which Ramses had traveled and, grasping the linen shroud on which he rested, gingerly slid him onto a sheet of Plexiglas *(opposite)*. Cut to fit inside the coffin, the plastic board made it easy for researchers to set Ramses on a surgical trolley at the beginning of each work session, then return him to the coffin when finished.

Additional restrictions forbade the researchers from taking tissue samples, no matter how tiny, from the pharaoh's body, but they were permitted to examine any loose material found in, on, or around the mummy. The linen shroud that lay under Ramses, a particularly rich source, was removed and marked with a rough grid corresponding to the mummy's anatomy. The sections were numbered and cut apart, then sealed in plastic bags and sent to laboratories for microscopic analysis. Technicians there identified around 60 species of fungi, most of which were growing in colonies in an area that team members guessed had remained unlighted and damp for years—the left side of Ramses' unwrapped back *(right, below)*. Later, when they examined the interior of the evisceration cavity, they located even more colonies of fungi, bringing the total to 370 and the number of species to 89.

At right, a specialist at the Museum of Man slides Ramses onto a sheet of Plexiglas while Lionel Balout, the project head, looks on. A piece of linen, stuffed inside the mummy at an undetermined but recent time, can be seen through the evisceration hole.

Below, a handful of the scientists involved in Operation Ramses gather around the pharaoh's mummy in the workroom in the Museum of Man on November 11, 1976. In all, more than 100 researchers took part in the project.

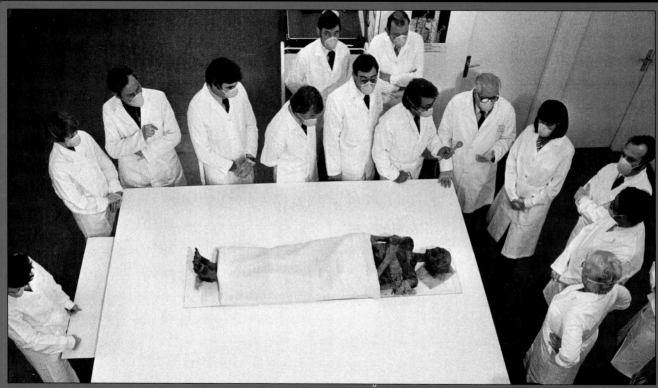

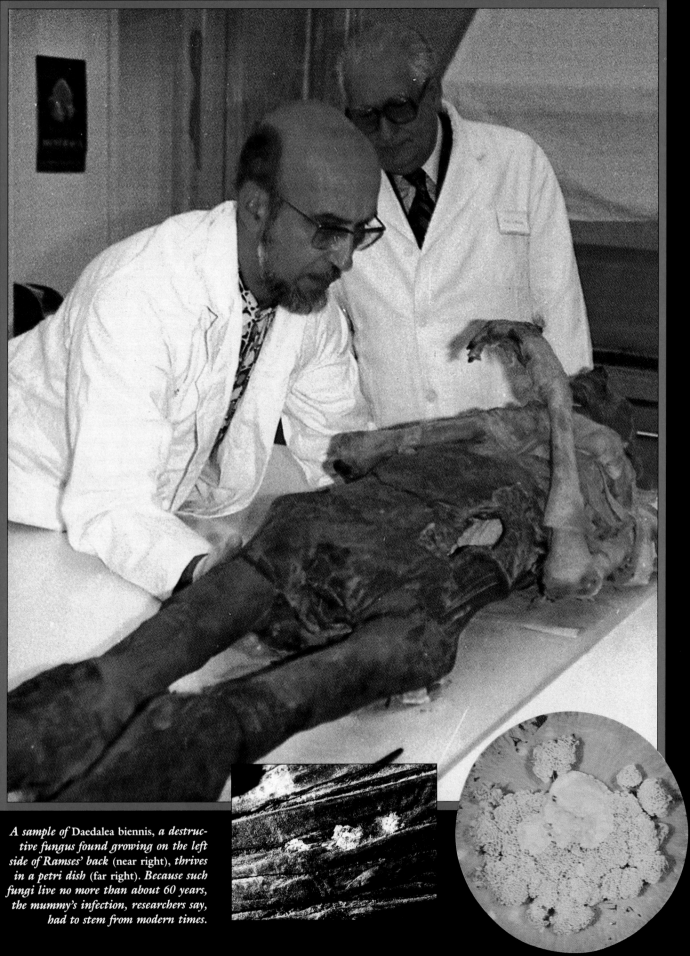

A sample of Daedalea biennis, *a destructive fungus found growing on the left side of Ramses' back (near right), thrives in a petri dish (far right). Because such fungi live no more than about 60 years, the mummy's infection, researchers say, had to stem from modern times.*

PORTRAITS OF THE PHARAOH AS AN OLD MAN

In their attempt to reveal lost secrets of the embalmers' art and to shed light on Ramses' physical condition during the last days of his life, the Paris researchers availed themselves of several modern tools. They used an endoscope, for example, to explore his abdominal cavity and a scanning electron microscope not only to study the structure and color of the pharaoh's hair *(opposite)* but also to uncover physical evidence concerning the ancient rescue and reburial of his mummy.

Sand discovered in and around the pharaoh's body, the microscope revealed, had features characteristic of grit found in both Upper and Lower Egypt but was also loaded with augites, green hornblendes, garnet,

zircon, and other minerals. Commonly found around Luxor in the south yet hardly ever in the area of Saqqara to the north, these substances, geologists explain, could only have come from Upper Egypt. The minerals probably entered the mummy sometime during the 21st Dynasty, when the high priests of Amen attempted to safeguard Ramses' mummy from desecration by graverobbers.

As shown on the following pages, the French researchers also made use of two innovative radiological techniques—xeroradiography and chromodensitography. A

combination of x-ray and photocopying technology, xeroradiography is ideally suited to the study of mummies, as it permits soft as well as hard body tissue to be recorded on film. Investigators made approximately 40 xeroradiographs of Ramses, including the one of his head below, which shows that the embalmers filled the pharaoh's nasal cavity with some sort of granular material, the exact nature of which remains unknown.

With chromodensitography, researchers are able to translate the lights, grays, and darks of a typical x-ray into a spectrum of colors. Used to create dramatic views of Ramses' head, neck, and thorax, the technique revealed for the first time that his neck was broken.

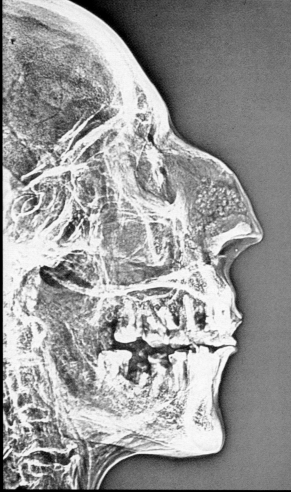

Stringy white patches just below Ramses' temple reveal hardening of the carotid artery, a sure sign of arteriosclerosis, in this xeroradiograph. The image also shows that the pharaoh's lower-right first molar is missing and that the jaw was abscessed, a painful condition that might have been caused by tooth decay or periodontal disease. Tiny, beadlike objects fill the nasal cavity, and an inch-long prosthesis seals the pharaoh's nostrils.

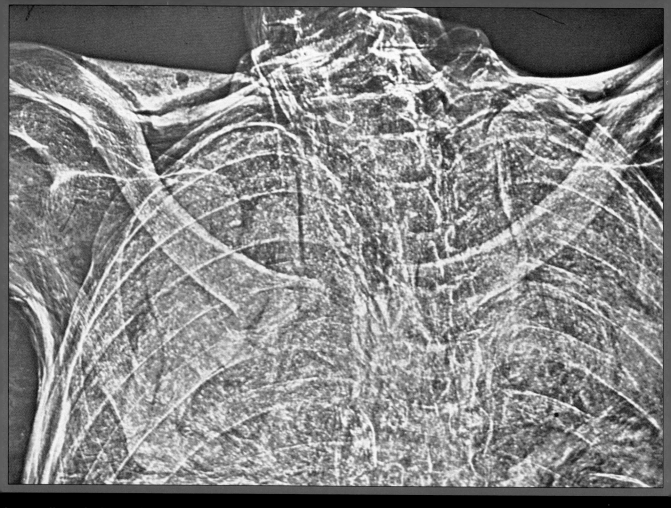

A xeroradiograph of Ramses' chest shows a pronounced curvature of the spine likely brought on by a disease called ankylosing spondylitis, or arthritis of the spine. The disorder affects the joints of the spinal column and pelvis and in time can lead to a complete loss of movement in these areas. The elderly Ramses, researchers speculate, not only walked hunched over but was probably unable to lift his head to look his successor in the eye.

At center in the chromodensitograph at left, a black gap between the fifth and sixth vertebrae marks a fracture of Ramses' spine. Experts believe the pharaoh's neck was broken during mummification, either accidentally—when embalmers allowed his head to fall back too far—or intentionally, as the embalmers may have

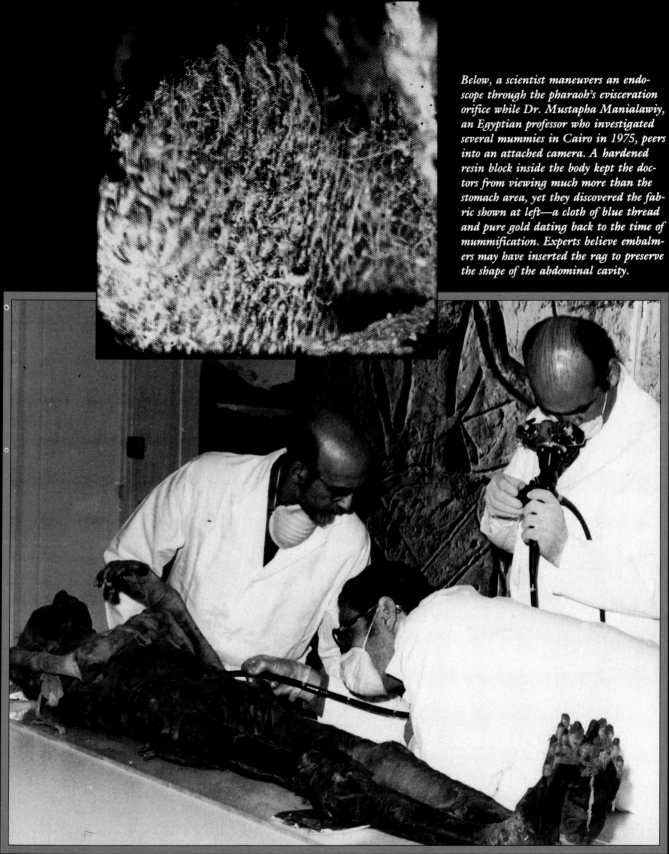

Below, a scientist maneuvers an endoscope through the pharaoh's evisceration orifice while Dr. Mustapha Manialawiy, an Egyptian professor who investigated several mummies in Cairo in 1975, peers into an attached camera. A hardened resin block inside the body kept the doctors from viewing much more than the stomach area, yet they discovered the fabric shown at left—a cloth of blue thread and pure gold dating back to the time of mummification. Experts believe embalmers may have inserted the rag to preserve the shape of the abdominal cavity.

After the scientists had finished investigating the mummy of Ramses II, conservators began the task of attending to a century's worth of degradations: cleaning and mending the few bandages that still clung to his fingers and toes *(below)*, patching some of the cracks running across his body, and restoring the coffin, transported separately from Cairo, in which Gaston Maspero had discovered the mummy at Deir el Bahari almost a century before.

Years older than Ramses, the casket was a magnificent specimen of late 18th-Dynasty workmanship. Except for a three-quarter-inch thick, arc-shaped strip of tamarisk that crowned the headpiece and about 20 four-inch-long pegs made

Thanks to conservators, 3,000-year-old bandages still bind the mummy's left hand and his feet. Experts removed the wrappings, which were covered with linen fibers, sand, and grit, dusted them, and carefully rewrapped them. Short and especially fragile pieces were stitched together with linen threads.

of ash, the casket had been built entirely from Lebanese cedar, a material used frequently in the tombs of the first kings of Egypt. Ancient carpenters had cut the wood into planks as much as three inches thick and six and a half feet long and masterfully bent them into gentle anthropoid curves. Dovetail joints were carved to lock the pieces together for what the workers believed would be eternity. But over the centuries, the C-shaped headpiece loosened, seams opened, a yard-long crack formed in the floor,

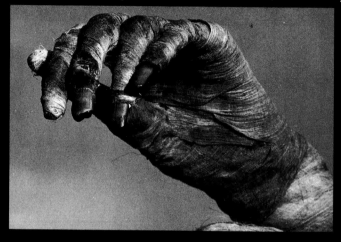

and a small, triangular chunk of wood broke away and was lost.

After sterilizing the coffin with ethylene-oxide gas, restorers filled in the crack with a mixture of vinyl glue and cedar dust, then replaced the missing fragment with a piece of old cedar from France's Limousin region. To ensure that the board blended in, the wood was deliberately cut so that its grain matched that of the rest of the wood, then painted with a light stain.

When Ramses' shroud-draped mummy was laid once more in the restored coffin *(right)*, one step remained before he could return home—a 12-hour shower of cobalt-60 gamma rays, delivered at a nuclear facility outside of Paris, to kill off the fungi that had attacked his body.

Ramses II (right) rests again in his coffin in Cairo's Egyptian Museum. The shroud around his shoulders is a 19th-Dynasty linen from the Egyptian Department of the Louvre Museum, which had been dusted and washed several times in distilled water before being gently placed around

AN INCOMPARABLE LITANY OF ACHIEVEMENT

Even to Ramses II Egypt was old. No nation ancient or modern boasts as long and fabled a history. The life-giving waters of the Nile spawned one of the world's earliest "cradles of civilization." During the fifth millennium BC, inhabitants of the Nile valley learned to rely on the recurring rhythm of the river's flooding to reap a bountiful harvest from the fertile land. By the end of the fourth millennium, permanent farming villages lined the narrow green corridor from Aswan to the delta.

As the population increased in the late fourth millennium, villages became towns, social stratification grew more pronounced as distinct classes emerged, and political power eventually coalesced into two autonomous kingdoms, Upper and Lower Egypt. Around 3100 BC the semilegendary ruler Menes united the country, thus becoming, in Egyptian tradition, Egypt's first pharaoh and inaugurating nearly three millennia of dynastic rule.

By about 2500 BC the pharaohs of what came to be called the Old Kingdom had acquired the status of living gods. Though they could not evade death in the mortal realm, their mummified remains were laid to rest in tombs built to last an eternity—the pyramids. Toward the end of the second millennium, the pharaohs' predominance was challenged by provincial nobles, and Egypt splintered into rival warring factions.

In 2040 BC King Nebhepetre Mentuhopte of Thebes ended the civil war and reasserted the primacy of the pharaoh by placing the everyday governance of the country in the hands of a bureaucracy beholden to him alone. His rule ushered in the Middle Kingdom, a time of cultural revival and political enlightenment. While still using the nation's treasure and manpower in the construction of tombs for themselves, the pharaohs also decreed public-works projects, such as drainage and irrigation, that benefited everyone.

By the 17th century BC, however, the Middle Kingdom in its turn fell into decline, leaving the country too weak to fend off the Hyksos—chariot-borne invaders from Palestine—who seized control of the delta. For the first time since dynastic rule began, a part of the country found itself under foreign domination.

The population chafed with anger and humiliation at this indignity. Nationalism finally grew into open revolt under the leadership of Thebes, which eventually expelled the Hyksos and ushered in Egypt's last golden age—the three dynasties that formed the New Kingdom.

18TH DYNASTY 1550-1307 BC

COLOSSI OF MEMNON

When Amosis I, founder of the 18th Dynasty, captured the Hyksos capital at Avaris and reunited the country, Egypt regained its self-respect. Amosis and his immediate successors began to reassert Egypt's role as a world power, pushing their armies into Palestine and up the Nile deep into Nubia. Internally, the period was marked by a cultural renaissance and a great increase in temple construction, especially at Karnak. The pharaoh Thutmose I began the custom, continued throughout the New Kingdom, of building his tomb across from Thebes in the Valley of the Kings.

Under Thutmose III, a brilliant military strategist, Egypt's empire expanded greatly, from the Euphrates to the fourth cataract of the Nile. Tribute from subjugated princes—as well as a rich variety of ideas and styles from numerous cultures—flowed into an increasingly cosmopolitan Egypt.

The 18th Dynasty reached its zenith under the master builder Amenhotep III. The magnificent Temple of Luxor and the enormous seated statues of himself *(above)* are but two of the works he commissioned. His son and heir, however, became the most controversial pharaoh in Egypt's history. Amenhotep IV encouraged a new, more realistic school of painting and sculpture, but far more significant were the extraordinary changes he wrought in the religious life of his people. He banned Egypt's powerful polytheistic establishment in favor of a single, omnipotent deity—the Aten, manifested in a radiating sun's disk. The pharaoh changed his own name to Akhenaten and, to distance himself from the entrenched priests of Thebes, built a new capital, which he called Akhetaten. Meanwhile, many of Egypt's vassals slipped away from the preoccupied pharaoh and fell under the influence of a new world power on the scene: the Hittites of Asia Minor.

Egypt's problems were exacerbated by a succession struggle when Akhenaten died. The throne eventually passed to the boy-king Tutankhamen, who produced no heir, then to a series of nonroyal military men who sought to erase Akhenaten's religious legacy. One of these generals, Horemheb, who also died childless, was the last pharaoh of the 18th Dynasty.

19TH DYNASTY
1307-1196 BC

TEMPLE AT ABU SIMBEL

20TH DYNASTY
1196-1070 BC

MEDINET HABU

On Horemheb's death, another soldier, Ramses I, became pharaoh and founder of the 19th Dynasty. At home he continued the process of undoing the damage caused by Akhenaten, whose reign was viewed as nothing less than a national catastrophe. In addition, Ramses longed to restore Egypt's tarnished imperial prestige, as in the glory days of Thutmose III and Amenhotep III.

Perhaps just as important for the well-being of the country, Ramses I produced an heir, thereby establishing a new royal bloodline. The pharaoh's reign was brief, but his son Seti I proved to be a strong ruler, inheriting his father's military prowess and political pragmatism. He put down an uprising in Nubia, turned back Libyan invaders in the delta, and reestablished an Egyptian presence in the Levant in the face of the expanding Hittite Empire. His prodigious program of temple construction further cemented the powerful priesthood's loyalty to the pharaoh. The country's prospects at home and abroad were bright when, on Seti's death, the throne passed to his son Ramses II.

Egypt's most renowned pharaoh ably carried on the legacy of his father and grandfather. He established a new capital at the family's ancestral home in the delta, from which he launched a campaign against the Hittites, culminating in the battle of Kadesh. Later, the pharaoh brokered a peace treaty that benefited both of the parties. Domestically, Ramses II reigned supreme, his authority unchallenged. His unparalleled building spree, while paying due homage to the major gods, also filled the country with colossal images of the pharaoh himself (*above*).

By the time Ramses died at the age of about 90, he had outlived 12 sons. The 13th, Merenptah, became pharaoh at an advanced age and immediately faced a series of foreign crises. He quelled revolts in the Levant and decisively defeated another Libyan incursion. But his decade-long reign was followed by another interval, from which historical records are spotty, of intrigue and conflicting claims to the throne. Several pharaohs—including a woman, Tausert—reigned briefly while civil war again wracked the land as the 19th Dynasty came to an end.

The origins of the 20th Dynasty are as murky as the demise of the 19th. The first pharaoh of the new line, Sethnakht, about whom scant knowledge has survived, could accomplish little in his two years on the throne other than to bequeath the country to his son Ramses III. This pharaoh, in some measure at least, restored to Egypt the glories of the New Kingdom. Early in his reign, Ramses III successfully fended off yet more assaults on the delta by the Libyans and the so-called Sea Peoples. With Egypt's borders secured, a limited degree of prosperity returned to the land, and Ramses III could, like his famous namesake, turn his attention to monument building. His most impressive accomplishment in this regard was his own mortuary temple (*above*).

But Ramses III's reign, in a sense, marked the last hurrah for the New Kingdom—and for Egypt itself as a dominant and vigorous power. Domestically, the economy was neither as sound nor the mood of the people as tranquil as Ramses may have portrayed them on steles and on the walls of Medinet Habu. Strikes by the royal tomb workers are indicative of the unrest that was simmering below the surface. Most troubling of all, however, are reports surviving on papyrus of an attempt on Ramses' life by members of his own harem. The result of this attempted coup d'état is unclear, but it is known that Ramses died a short time later and the throne passed to his son Ramses IV.

Seven subsequent pharaohs—all of them named Ramses—completed the 20th Dynasty. Their reigns became a litany of inexorable decline. Egypt's empire was gone; invaders were at the gates, and this time they would not be stopped. Even the Nile seems to have turned its back on the country as year after year of low floods produced poor harvests. Coupled with widespread official corruption, the result was shortage, then famine. Tomb robbing became rampant, and civil order broke down.

Although 10 more dynasties followed, the next seven centuries included periods of chaos, internecine war, and spells of foreign occupation. In 332 BC Alexander the Great's conquest of Egypt finally ended the long line of Egyptian pharaohs.

ACKNOWLEDGMENTS

The editors wish to thank the following individuals and institutions for their valuable assistance in the preparation of this volume:

Mahasti Afshar, The Getty Conservation Institute, Marina del Rey, California; Carol Andrews, Department of Egyptian Antiquities, British Museum, London; Ibrahim Bakr, Egyptian Antiquities Organization, Cairo; Peter F. Dorman, The Oriental Institute, University of Chicago, Chicago; Trude Dothan, Hebrew University Archeology Institute, Jerusalem; Richard Fazzini, Brooklyn Museum, Brooklyn; Dennis C. Forbes, San Francisco; Monique Gehrke, Alexandria, Virginia; April Goebel, National

Geographic Society, Washington, D.C.; Ali Hassan, Egyptian Antiquities Organization, Cairo; Nasri Iskandar, Egyptian Museum Cairo, Cairo; Barry Iverson, Cairo; John Larson, The Oriental Institute, University of Chicago, Chicago; Shin Maekawa, The Getty Conservation Institute, Marina del Rey, California; G. T. Martin, Department of Egyptology, University College, London; Myron Marx, Department of Radiology, California Pacific Medical Center, San Francisco; O. Louis Mazzatenta, National Geographic Society, Washington, D.C.; Gerhard Prause, Hamburg; Edgar B. Pusch, Roemer and Pelizaeus Museum, Hildesheim, Germany; Régis Ramière, Centre d'Etudes Nucléaires,

Grenoble; Ann M. Roth, Philadelphia; Colette Roubet, Professeur, Muséum National d'Histoire Naturelle, Chaire de Préhistoire, Paris; Anna Maria Donadoni Roveri, Museo Egizio, Turin; Mohammad Saleh, Egyptian Museum Cairo, Cairo; Lisa Snider, The Oriental Institute, University of Chicago, Chicago; Pat Spencer, The Egyptian Exploration Society, London; Emily Teeter, The Oriental Institute, University of Chicago, Chicago; Christian Thorin, Washington, D.C.; Elisabetta Valtz, Museo Egizio, Turin; Sylvia Wiens, The Egyptian Exploration Society, London; Joachim Willeitner, Verlag Philipp von Zabern, Mainz, Germany; Jean Yoyotte, Collège de France, Paris.

PICTURE CREDITS

BIBLIOGRAPHY

BOOKS

Andrews, Carol. *Ancient Egyptian Jewellery*. London: British Museum, 1990.

Arnold, Dieter. *Building in Egypt: Pharaonic Stone Masonry*. New York: Oxford University Press, 1991.

Baedeker's Egypt. Englewood Cliffs, N.J.: Prentice-Hall, 1984.

Baines, John, and Jaromír Málek. *The Cultural Atlas of the World: Ancient Egypt*. Alexandria, Va.: Stonehenge, 1990.

Balout, Doyen Lionel. *La Momie de Ramsès II*. Paris: Éditions Recherche sur les Civilisations, 1985.

Belzoni, Giovanni Batista. *Egypt and Nubia*. London: John Murray, 1822.

Bierbrier, Morris. *The Tomb-Builders of the Pharaohs*. London: British Museum, 1982.

Breasted, James Henry. *Ancient Records of Egypt* (Vol. 3). Chicago: University of Chicago Press, 1906.

Bucaille, Maurice. *Mummies of the Pharaohs: Modern Medical Investigations*. New York: St. Martin's Press, 1990.

Bunson, Margaret. *The Encyclopedia of Ancient Egypt*. New York: Facts On File, 1991.

Cambridge Ancient History (Vol. 2), 1973.

Corzo, Miguel Angel, and Mahasti Afshar (Eds.). *Art and Eternity: The Nefertari Wall Paintings Conservation Project, 1986-1992*. Los Angeles: The Getty Conservation Institute and the Egyptian Antiquities Organization, in press.

Cott, Jonathan. *The Search for Omm Sety: A Story of Eternal Love*. New York: Doubleday, 1987.

David, A. Rosalie:
The Ancient Egyptians: Religious Beliefs and Practices. London: Routledge & Kegan Paul, 1982.
The Egyptian Kingdoms. New York: Peter Bedrick Books, 1988.
A Guide to Religious Ritual at Abydos. Warminster, Wiltshire: Aris & Phillips, 1981.

Delacampagne, Christian. *Immortelle Égypte*. Paris: Éditions Nathan, 1990.

Dothan, Trude, and Moshe Dothan. *People of the Sea: The Search for the Philistines*. New York: Macmillan, 1992.

Egypt: Land of the Pharaohs (Lost Civilizations series). Alexandria, Va.: Time-Life Books, 1992.

El Mahdy, Christine. *Mummies, Myth and Magic in Ancient Egypt*. New York: Thames and Hudson, 1989.

Freed, Rita E. *Ramesses the Great*. Memphis, Tenn.: City of Memphis, Tennessee, and the Egyptian Antiquities Organization, in cooperation with Memphis Brooks Museum of Art and the Institute of Egyptian Art and Archaeology, Memphis State University, 1987.

Golvin, Jean-Claude, and Jean-Claude Goyon. *Karnak, Ägypten: Anatomie eines Tempels*. Tübingen, Germany: Ernst Wasmuth, 1990.

Greener, Leslie. *The Discovery of Egypt*. New York: Dorset Press, 1960.

Harris, James E., and Edward F. Wente (Eds.). *An X-Ray Atlas of the Royal Mummies*. Chicago: University of Chicago Press, 1980.

Hayes, William C. *Glazed Tiles from a Palace of Ramesses II at Kantir*. New York: Metropolitan Museum of Art, 1937.

Hicks, Jim, and the Editors of Time-Life Books. *The Empire Builders* (Emergence of Man series). New York: Time-Life Books, 1974.

Hölscher, Uvo:
Medinet Habu Studies, 1924-28: The Architectural Survey of the Great Temple and Palace of Medinet Habu. Oriental Institute Communication No. 5. Chicago: University of Chicago Press, 1929.
Medinet Habu Studies, 1928/29: The Architectural Survey. Oriental Institute Communication No. 7. Chicago: University of Chicago Press, 1930.
The Mortuary Temple of Ramses III (Vol. 3, part 1, of *The Excavation of Medinet Habu*). Translated by Mrs. Keith C. Seele. Chicago: University of Chicago Press, 1941.
The Mortuary Temple of Ramses III (Vol. 4, part 2, of *The Excavation of Medinet Habu*). Translated by Elizabeth B. Hauser. Chicago: University of Chicago Press, 1951.

Hornung, Erik. *The Valley of the Kings: Horizon of Eternity*. Translated by David Warburton. New York: Timken, 1990.

An Introduction to Ancient Egypt. London: British Museum, 1979.

James, T. G. H.:
Ancient Egypt: The Land and Its Legacy. London: British Museum, 1988.
Egyptian Painting and Drawing in the British Museum. London: British Museum, 1985.

James, T. G. H., and W. V. Davies. *Egyptian Sculpture*. London: British Museum, 1991.

Kemp, Barry J. *Ancient Egypt: Anatomy of a Civilization*. New York: Routledge, 1989.

Kitchen, K. A.:
Pharaoh Triumphant: The Life and Times of Ramesses II, King of Egypt. Warminster, Wiltshire: Aris & Phillips, 1982.
The Third Intermediate Period in Egypt. Warminster, Wiltshire: Aris & Phillips, 1973.

Lesko, Barbara S. *The Remarkable Women of Ancient Egypt*. Berkeley, Calif.: B.C. Scribe, 1978.

Lloyd, Seton, and Hans Wolfgang Müller. *Ancient Architecture*. New York: Rizzoli, 1986.

Lurker, Manfred. *The Gods and Symbols of Ancient Egypt: An Illustrated Dictionary*. London: Thames and Hudson, 1980.

MacQuitty, William:
Abu Simbel. New York: G. P. Putnam, 1965.
Ramesses the Great: Master of the World. New York: Crown, 1978.

Manniche, Lise. *Sexual Life in Ancient Egypt*. New York: KPI, 1987.

Martin, Geoffrey T. *The Hidden Tombs of Memphis*. London: Thames and Hudson, 1991.

Maspero, Gaston:
Guide to the Cairo Museum (2d ed.). Translated by J. E. Quibell and

A. A. Quibell. Cairo: Printing Office of the French Institute of Oriental Archaeology, 1905.

Le Musée Égyptien Recueil de Monuments et de Notices sur les Fouilles d'Égyote. Cairo: D'Archéologie Oriental, 1907.

Michalowski, Kazimierz. *Art of Ancient Egypt.* Translated by Norbert Guterman. New York: Harry N. Abrams, 1969.

Milton, Joyce. *Sunrise of Power.* New York: HBJ Press, 1980.

Montet, Pierre:

Everyday Life in Egypt in the Days of Ramesses the Great. Philadelphia: University of Pennsylvania Press, 1981.

Lives of the Pharaohs. Cleveland: World Publishing, 1968.

National Geographic Society. *Ancient Egypt: Discovering Its Splendors.* Washington, D.C.: National Geographic Society, 1978.

Newby, P. H. *Warrior Pharaohs: The Rise and Fall of the Egyptian Empire.* London: Faber and Faber, 1980.

Prause, Gerhard. *Spurender Geschichte.* Munich: Droemersche Verlagsanstalt T. H. Knaur Nacht, 1991.

Quirke, Stephen, and Jeffrey Spencer (Eds.). *The British Museum Book of Ancient Egypt.* New York: Thames and Hudson, 1992.

Rainey, Anson F. (Ed.). *Egypt, Israel, Sinai: Archaeological and Historical Relationships in the Biblical Period.* Tel Aviv: Tel Aviv University, 1987.

Ramses le Grand. Paris: Galeries Nationales du Grand Palais, 1976.

Reeves, C. N. (Ed.). *After Tut'ankhamun: Research and Excavation in the Royal Necropolis at Thebes.* London: Kegan Paul, 1992.

Reeves, Nicholas. *The Complete Tutankhamun: The King, the Tomb, the Royal Treasure.* London: Thames and Hudson, 1990.

Romer, John:

Ancient Lives: Daily Life in Egypt of the Pharaohs. New York: Holt, Rinehart and Winston, 1984.

Valley of the Kings. New York: William Morrow, 1981.

Saleh, Mohamed, and Hourig Sourouzian. *The Egyptian Museum Cairo.* Mainz, Germany: Organisation of Egyptian Antiquities, The Arabian Republic of Egypt, 1987.

Sandars, N. K. *The Sea Peoples: Warriors of the Ancient Mediterranean, 1250-1150 BC.* London: Thames and Hudson, 1985.

Smith, G. Elliot. *Catalogue Général des Antiquités Égyptiennes du Musée du Caire, Volume 59: The Royal Mummies.* Cairo: Service des Antiquités de l'Égypte, 1912.

Stead, Miriam. *Egyptian Life.* London: British Museum, 1986.

Strouhal, Eugen. *Life in Ancient Egypt.* Cambridge: Cambridge University Press, 1992.

Trigger, B. G., B. J. Kemp, D. O'Connor, and A. B. Lloyd. *Ancient Egypt: A Social History.* Cambridge: Cambridge University Press, 1983.

Uphill, E. P. *The Temples of Per Ramesses.* Warminster, Wiltshire: Aris and Phillips, 1984.

Watterson, Barbara. *Women in Ancient Egypt.* New York: St. Martin's Press, 1991.

Wente, Edward F. *Letters from Ancient Egypt.* Atlanta: Scholars Press, 1990.

West, John Anthony. *The Traveler's Key to Ancient Egypt.* New York: Alfred A. Knopf, 1985.

Who Was Who 1929-1940 (Vol. 3). London: Adam & Charles Black, 1967.

Wilkinson, Alix. *Ancient Egyptian Jewellery.* London: Methuen, 1971.

PERIODICALS

Archaeology. Vol. 44, no. 6, 1991.

Balout, Doyen Lionel. "Ramses II au Musée de l'Homme." *Archeologia,* February 1978.

Bell, Lanny. "The Oriental Institute's Epigraphic Survey." *KMT,* Fall 1990.

Brock, Edwin. "Piecing It All Together." *KMT,* Spring 1991.

Casson, Lionel. "Ancient Naval Warfare." *MHQ: The Quaterly Journal of Military History.* Autumn 1991.

Dothan, Trude. "Last Outpost of the Egyptian Empire." *National Geographic,* December 1982.

Gerster, Georg. "Abu Simbel's Ancient Temples Reborn." *National Geographic,* May 1969.

Gore, Rick. "Ramses the Great." *National Geographic,* April 1991.

Harell, James A., and V. Max Brown. "The Oldest Surviving Topographical Map from Ancient Egypt (Turin Papyri 1879, 1899, and 1969)." *Journal of the American Research Center in Egypt,* Vol. 29, 1992.

Journal of Egyptian Archaeology, Vol. 39, 1953.

Klink, Renate. "German Egyptologist Edgar Pusch Reveals Results of 12-Year Dig." *Hildesheimer Allgemeine Zeitung,* Dec. 31, 1992.

Leclant, Jean, and Catherine Berger. "Champollion Mémoires d'Egypte." *Archeologia,* February 1991.

"My Buffalo or Ancient Rocks?" *Egyptian Gazette,* May 11, 1993.

Pusch, Edgar B.:

"Bericht über die Sechste Hauptkampagne in Qantir-Piramesse/Nord, Herbst 1988." *Göttinger Miszellen* (Institut für Ägyptologie, Göttingen, Germany), 1989, Vol. 112, pp. 67-90.

"Metallverarbeitende Werkstätten der Frühen Ramessidenzeit in Qantir-Piramesse/Nord. Ein Zwischenbericht." *Ägypten und Levante* (Wiener Akademie der Wissenschaften, Vienna), 1990, Vol. 1, pp.75-113 (supplement).

Rutherford, John B. "Why Save the Tomb of Rameses II?" *KMT,* Fall 1990.

OTHER SOURCES

Dorman, Peter F. "The Epigraphic Survey." *Annual Report, 1990-1991,* The Oriental Institute.

Gaballa Ali Gaballa. "Nefertari: For Whom the Sun Shines." First progress report on the wall paintings of the tomb of Nefertari. The Egyptian Antiquities Organization and the Getty Conservation Institute, July 1987.

"In the Tomb of Nefertari: Conservation of the Wall Paintings." Catalog. Santa Monica: J. Paul Getty Museum, 1992.

"Preliminary Report on the Excavations in Akhmim by the Egyptian Antiquities Organization." Report. Cairo: Service des Antiquités, IFAO, 1983.

Pusch, Edgar B.:
"Pi-Ramesse-Geliebt von Amun, Hauptquartier Deiner Streitwagentruppen." Pelizaeus-Museum Hildesheim, Die Ägyptische Sammlung. Catalog. Mainz: Philipp von Zabern Verlag, 1993.

"Recent Work at Northern Piramesse, 1986." *Fragments of a*

Shattered Visage. The Proceedings of the International Symposium on Ramesses the Great, 1991. Memphis, Tenn.: Institute of Egyptian Art and Archaeology, 1993.

"Valley of the Kings Preservation Project." Proposal. Luxor, Egypt: Rutherford & Chekene, Consulting Engineers, San Francisco, 1991.

INDEX

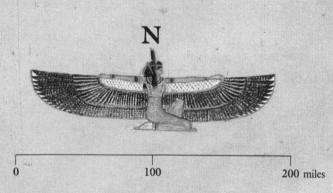

LIBYA

N

0   100   200 miles

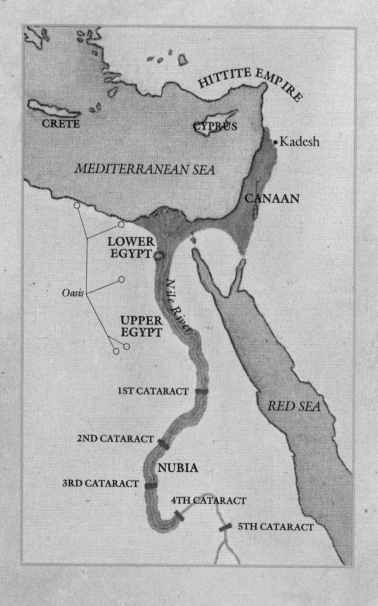

CRETE

HITTITE EMPIRE

CYPRUS

• Kadesh

MEDITERRANEAN SEA

CANAAN

WESTERN
DESERT

LOWER
EGYPT

Oasis

Nile River

UPPER
EGYPT

1ST CATARACT

RED SEA

2ND CATARACT

NUBIA

3RD CATARACT

4TH CATARACT

5TH CATARACT